The Bible:
A Modern
Jewish Approach

The Bible:
A Modern
Jewish Approach

by Bernard J. Bamberger

SECOND EDITION

SCHOCKEN BOOKS · NEW YORK

This volume is one of a series of "Hillel Little Books." Developed by the B'nai B'rith Hillel Foundations, the books in this series deal with issues of fundamental importance to Jewish college students. Written by men of variant points of view, they are intended to stimulate further study and discussion.

DEDICATED TO THE MEMORY OF

REBECCA RABINOFF KAPLAN

1902–1954

IN REVERENCE AND AFFECTION

CONTENTS

The Bible:

A Modern

Jewish Approach

I

THE QUESTION

What meaning, what value does the Bible have for the modern man — in particular, for the modern Jew?

Such a question has little point for those who are convinced in advance that the Bible is the product of supernatural revelation. If God has explicitly declared His will for us, and if the Bible is the authentic record of His commandments, we need not discuss their relevance. Our task is simply to try to understand and to obey.

Another group of dogmatists may also be inclined to brush our question aside: those who are convinced in advance that the Bible is a collection of old wives' tales, unworthy of serious consideration by the enlightened. The Bible does contain pages which are contradicted by the generally accepted findings of modern science. It seems strange that, a century after Darwin, this fact should still come as something of a shock to many students. But though the Bible stems from a pre-scientific age, should we hastily discard it as valueless? The scientific temper would require us rather to approach this massive historical monument with objectivity and to examine it with precision and thoroughness.

And such is the intent of this essay. We shall not assume here that the Bible is the inscrutable record of divine revelation, nor that it is "merely" this or that.

We shall try to approach it fairly and honestly and see what it has to say to us.

In this essay, the word *Bible* and its equivalents will mean the Hebrew Bible which both Jews and Christians accept as sacred scripture. It is what Christians call the Old Testament, since for them the term Bible also includes the New Testament. Our inquiry will not extend to the latter. We are not passing judgment on the value of the New Testament, nor shall we explain in this context why the Jews have not admitted it into their sacred writings. It is simply not the subject of discussion here.

Our study should lead us finally to confront a basic issue: the *personal relation* of the modern reader to the Bible. For previous generations, and for many millions today, it is not just a book like other books. (This fact itself requires thoughtful consideration.) But if we do not make an initial assumption about the divine origin and authority of the Bible, does it still have a special, contemporary, personal relevance for us? Or is it at most an interesting collection of ancient documents?

The individual must ultimately decide this question for himself. This essay is an attempt to state the problem plainly, to clear away some of the confusion that might otherwise trouble the reader, to supply a necessary background of information, and to make some suggestions that may help him in arriving at his own conclusions.

But before we can deal with the crucial issue, we must make a considerable circuit. Other matters must first engage our attention. For even if the Bible had no significant message for our time, it would not be unimportant. The Bible, by general agreement, is a classic.

II

THE BIBLE IN WESTERN CIVILIZATION

One is tempted to define a classic as a book we feel we ought to read — but would rather not! In fact, a classic often demands a little extra effort from us at the start, but yields fuller and more lasting pleasure than "light reading." Courses in "The Great Books" are sometimes surprisingly enjoyable. More formally, however, a classic is a work that has been incorporated into the cultural heritage of a people and has exercised a continuing influence.

Some books are classics because in their time they inaugurated new ways of thinking. Most classics of science are of this sort. You would hardly study medicine today from the writings of Galen, or chemistry from the monographs of Priestley. Though these books are classics, their interest is primarily historical. Whatever is of permanent value in them has been absorbed into the books that have superseded them.

Occasionally a classic whose subject matter is dated may survive because of its literary charm. But real literature possesses more than verbal excellence. The great books, though they may have been written far away and long ago, though they may contain much that is alien to our experience and ways of thinking, deal with aspects of human life so fundamental and so perennial that they still have power to stir our emotions. Homer's appeal to the modern reader is not only his powerful diction and noble rhythms. For though we are not much interested in elaborate armor or feasts of whole roasted oxen, our hearts ache as old Priam pleads for the release of his son's body, and thrill as Odysseus desperately matches his intelligence against the stupid strength of the Cyclops.

The Bible is certainly a classic in more than the historical sense. Anyone who reads the story of Joseph (Genesis, chapters 37, 39–45) will agree that it is first rate narrative prose; nor can one fail to perceive the lyric power of David's lament over Saul and Jonathan (II Samuel, chapter 1). The merit of these two selections lies not only in the vigor and conciseness of the writing, but in the intensity of human feeling that suffuses them.

Classics, we observed, have a continuing influence on culture. Homer's epics not only inspired the drama, painting, and sculpture of ancient Greece, but powerfully affected Latin, medieval, and modern culture. (A recent musical play retold the tale of Troy against a rural American background). Yet wide and pervasive as these influences have been, they are slight in comparison with the impact of the Bible on human civilization.

This impact derives partly from the fact that the

Bible has been translated into virtually all languages. The importance of translation for the spread of culture is something we do not often think about, perhaps because it is so obvious. Now the first ambitious and widely disseminated translation of which we have record was the Greek rendering of the Bible (the Septuagint), made by Jews in Alexandria in the centuries prior to the Christian era. The process of Bible translation has been going on ever since. The first literary monument in many a language has been a Bible version, which set the standard for style in that tongue. This does not apply only to the more backward peoples. Luther's rendering of the Bible is generally recognized as the chief force in creating the modern German language. The King James version of 1611 has profoundly modified English style and usage. Such Hebrew idioms as "the skin of my teeth" (Job 19.20) and "a land flowing with milk and honey" (Exodus 3.8) have been naturalized in our language. The impact of the Biblical style on writers of English has often been noted: Abraham Lincoln comes to mind at once.

Biblical subject matter has been an inexhaustible resource for creative artists. To list examples would be wearisome. We think immediately of Milton's *Paradise Lost* and Thomas Mann's *Joseph* trilogy; of Racine's *Athalie* and *Esther* and Marc Conolly's tender play, *The Green Pastures;* of Michelangelo's Moses and many of Rembrandt's finest canvasses; of Handel's oratorios, Honegger's *King David*, and Stravinsky's *Symphony of Psalms*. Liturgical music (which includes some of the greatest masterpieces ever composed) is largely set to texts from the Hebrew Bible. The *Sanctus* is Isaiah 6.3; the *Benedictus*, Psalm 118.26.

Even were we to list all the poems, plays, novels, operas, and other major works based on Biblical themes, we should not have measured the extent to which the Bible has influenced literature. The late Dr. Solomon Goldman published over six hundred pages of "Echoes and Allusions" to the Book of Genesis, drawn from European and American writers. And even this bulky collection was little more than a sampling of the available material referring to a single Biblical book.

All this underscores the fact that one cannot understand Western culture without some knowledge of the Bible. But we still have not stated the main point. To grasp it, let us turn back briefly to Homer.

In the heyday of the classical civilization, Homer was the possession of all who spoke Greek. The Homeric poems were a kind of scripture, the subject-matter of elementary education, the theme of popular song and drama, a source of conversational commonplace. But with the breakdown of classical civilization, the Homeric influence was at an end. Its memory has persisted among the book-loving minority, the learned and literary élite, but only among them.

The Bible, however, though it was always the subject of scholarly concern, has constantly permeated the life of the masses. Even the unlettered man of the Middle Ages knew the Bible stories through the sermons he heard in church, and through their depiction in stone and stained glass. With the Protestant Reformation, the Bible rapidly became the book of the people. As printing made it more readily available, it found its way into homes where no other book was known. It was constantly read in family worship and by individuals seeking guidance and comfort. Robert Burns describes a familiar scene in the life of a poor Scotch family:

"The priest-like father reads the sacred page,
    How Abram was the friend of God on high;
Or Moses bade eternal warfare wage
With Amalek's ungracious progeny;
    Or how the royal bard did groaning lie
Beneath the stroke of Heaven's avenging ire;
    Or Job's pathetic plaint, and wailing cry;
Or rapt Isaiah's wild seraphic fire;
Or other holy seers that tune the sacred lyre."

Perhaps the most dramatic illustration is furnished by the Negro spirituals. Slaves kidnapped from the African jungles and carried off to servitude in the New World voiced their yearning for freedom by singing "Go Down, Moses" and uttered their faith in chants about Daniel and Joshua. American Negro poetry has few references to the Congo, but many to the Jordan.

The influence of the Bible on the life, thought, and character of individuals has been all-pervasive and incalculable. Its effect on society and its history can more readily be measured. The connection between the Bible and the Protestant Reformation has already been mentioned. The social and spiritual temper of sixteenth century Europe was such as to stimulate interest in the Bible. But it is equally clear that much of the energy that produced the Reformation came

7

from within the Bible itself. The results of this upheaval were not limited to the areas of Christian doctrine or ecclesiastical organization. Many types of social, political, and cultural change were set in motion at the time.

The reading of the Bible exerted a dynamic effect long after the Reformation had been consolidated. The multiplication of Protestant sects resulted largely from disagreements over the meaning of Scripture. Among the consequences was a recurrent tendency to stress the Hebraic element, sometimes leading to a lessened emphasis on specifically Christian concepts and values. The Mayflower Pilgrims established a commonwealth consciously modeled on the theocracy of ancient Israel. Hebrew studies were widely cultivated in early New England; Old Testament names were in general use; the Puritan Sabbath, in imitation of Jewish usage, was observed from evening to evening. (The Puritans, of course, kept Sunday in this fashion; but at a later date, the Seventh Day Baptists and Seventh Day Adventists reverted to the historical Sabbath).

It was doubtless just a happy coincidence that the Liberty Bell bore the inscription: "Proclaim liberty throughout the land unto all the inhabitants thereof" (Leviticus 25.9). But it was no accident that patriot preachers during the American Revolution compared George III to Pharaoh and George Washington to Moses, that Benjamin Franklin proposed that the Great Seal of the United States should depict Israel crossing the Red Sea, and that the opponents of slavery constantly quoted texts from the Five Books of Moses.

Some Puritan splinter-groups adopted so many Old Testament customs that they were stigmatized as Jews. The charge was probably not justified. But in nineteenth century Russia, an extensive Judaizing movement did occur. It was not the result of propaganda by living Jews; for it took place in the interior sections of the Empire from which Jews were excluded. Many plain folk, it seems, spent the long nights of the Russian winter reading the Bible aloud. And some of them were led, by their reading and discussion, to discard the New Testament in favor of the Old. The first stage in this process was to adopt Saturday as the Sabbath; a considerable group went on to complete and formal adoption of the Jewish religion.

In our own day, this history was repeated in the remote Italian village of San Nicandro. A peasant named Donato Manduzio, disabled by an injury in World War I, began to read a Bible he had obtained from a Protestant missionary. He became convinced of the truth of Judaism and won many of his fellow-villagers to his viewpoint. The group was formally admitted to the Jewish community in 1946; and after the death of Manduzio, emigrated *en masse* to Israel.

We have been describing the impact of Scripture on the Christian world. In Jewish life its effects have been less explosive because the Biblical influence was constant and all-pervasive. For two thousand years, most Jewish males knew the Bible and some of its simpler commentaries in the original. Hebrew learning was less common (though not unknown) among women; but translations or paraphrases of the Bible in the language of daily life were provided for their use. Copious selections from the Psalms and other Biblical books were included in the daily prayers. Sabbath and festival observance was closely bound up with Scriptural teaching. All the relationships of family, business, and community life were regulated by a legal system based on the Five Books of Moses. Scholarship and research centered on the same fundamental text. Grammarians, lexicographers and commentators in Spain and France sought an exact comprehension of Scriptural language. Legalists tried to determine the implications and applications of the Biblical commandments. Philosophers and mystics labored over proof that their novel theories were already suggested in the words of Scripture. When Mohammed called the Jews "the People of the Book," when Heine referred to the Bible as a "portable Fatherland," they dealt more in truth than in poetry.

What, then, is the secret of the vitality of the Bible, so constant through changing centuries? How did it exert such dynamic power on so many ages and peoples? What did it offer them? Does it still have something important to say to the men and women of the twentieth century?

Again we postpone the attempt at an answer while we add a new dimension to our inquiry.

III

THE REDISCOVERY OF
THE BIBLICAL WORLD

Among the outstanding achievements of the human
intellect we must class the reconstruction of the history
and culture of the ancient Near East. The grandeur of
Egypt had, indeed, never been forgotten: the Pyramids
and other towering structures were visible testimony
to superb skill in engineering, architecture, and the
decorative arts. Some records of the might and civilization of Babylonia, Assyria, and Phoenicia were pre-
served by ancient historians, and the glories of old
Persia were still remembered. But the great Hittite
Empire in Asia Minor had been completely obliterated
from history; and until one hundred and fifty years
ago, our notions even about Egypt and Babylon were
fragmentary and largely erroneous.

In our time, a large part of the story of the origins
of civilization has been recovered. Archaeology, no
longer a promiscuous hunt for buried treasure, but an
exact and disciplined science, has laid bare all sorts of
structures, from fortresses and palaces to industrial
works and peasants' huts. Expert investigators have
identified the tools and utensils, fabrics, pottery, jew-
elry, cosmetic materials, art objects, and religious
symbols of forgotten peoples. Forms of writing obsolete for thousands of years have been deciphered by
methods akin to those used to "break" a secret code;

and dozens of long dead languages have come at least to a dusty half-life.

The written records are abundant. Royal inscriptions, law codes, mythological and ritual texts, historical chronicles, personal and official letters, business documents, magical amulets, schoolboy exercises — inscribed on clay, stone, or papyrus — are now available to students. On the basis of all the evidence, written and otherwise, we have gained a far broader and more exciting picture of ancient history.

The investigation of the ancient Near Eastern languages, literature, and culture is an important branch of humane studies, worth pursuing for itself. But it has been of particular interest to students of the Bible. For the new discoveries give us a wealth of information about the neighbors of ancient Israel and fill out the background of the Scriptural story. Archaeological data have clarified the problems of Biblical research and helped us to understand many a difficult sentence of the sacred text.

But while the recent discoveries have shed much light on the Bible, some experts have utilized the new material to cast a kind of shadow over the Scriptures. For archaeology has substantiated more fully what the Bible itself makes plain: that the civilizations of the Nile and Euphrates valleys are far older than the Biblical writings or the events the latter record. Abraham, we read in Genesis, was born in the city of Ur. This city, excavated in recent decades, was the seat of an advanced culture centuries before the probable time of Abraham. Egypt had a history of perhaps two thousand years when Moses organized his revolt. Was it not plausible that the Hebrews, living in these ancient and highly civilized empires, should have derived their religious and ethical ideas from their environment?

Such suggestions had been made long before on the basis of guess-work. Now it was thought that they were actually demonstrable. Two factors must be recognized: natural enthusiasm over newly reclaimed treasures, and the unmistakable anti-Jewish prejudice of some of the savants. It was announced in various quarters that the Israelites were little more than second-hand dealers in religion and morality. The religious and ethical concepts, the tales and legends, the legal provisions found in Scripture were borrowed from Egypt or Babylonia!

The student who would like to examine these claims for himself is now in position to do so. The Babylonian epics, the Code of Hammurabi, Ikh-enaton's Hymn to the Sun God, and the other alleged sources of the Hebrew writers have now been assembled in one massive volume, in English translations prepared by outstanding Orientalists.* Anyone who has the stamina to read through these records can form his own conclusions. He will find a few cases in which the Biblical authors undoubtedly borrowed literary motifs and even phrases from earlier sources. He will recognize a number of parallels (not as many as the index of the volume suggests), some of which perhaps are not

---

*Ancient Near Eastern Texts Relating to the Old Testament, edited by James B. Pritchard. Princeton University Press, 1950.

accidental. But he will also discover such fundamental differences of outlook, content, spirit and style as underscore more plainly than ever the originality of the Biblical writers.

The ancient Israelites were in no way isolated from other peoples and their cultures. Palestine, the bridge between Asia and Africa, has been through most of its history subject to one or another of the great powers. When armies were not maneuvering over the land of Israel, caravans were traversing it. Archaeological excavations in Palestine reveal a material culture that was dominated by foreign influences. The pottery, carved ivories, signets, household decorations, and other surviving artifacts of the ancient Hebrews are generally mediocre, and at best are good copies of Egyptian or other foreign models. Solomon's temple, the Bible itself states, was planned and built by a Phoenician architect. The fortifications of Israelite cities were neither as massive nor as well constructed as earlier walls built on the same sites by previous inhabitants of Canaan.

The ancient Israelites were not distinguished for technical, commercial, maritime, military, or artistic skills.* Yet the writings they produced are unique in

*Such statements should not be pressed too far. The Israelites were by no means primitive incompetents. The tunnel cut through solid rock to bring water from the pool of Siloam into Jerusalem (II Chron. 32.30), through which water still flows, is evidence that King Hezekiah had skilled engineers; and the copper smeltery built on the shores of the Red Sea under King Solomon's direction (excavated in 1938 and succeeding years by Dr. Nelson Glueck) was part of a highly organized industrial

their lofty spiritual outlook and incomparable for beauty of expression.

Let us see some of the ways in which the Bible differs from other literature of the ancient East.

IV

CHALLENGE TO TYRANTS

The old Oriental writings breathe the spirit of despotism. The king is, at the least, the designated representative of the god. The Code of King Hammurabi is inscribed on the sides of a stone column; the upper part of the shaft depicts the monarch receiving the laws from the hand of the sun god. The Assyrian kings present themselves as the beloved favorites of Asshur, the national deity; it is in obedience to his command that they embark on their conquests.

This tendency reached its fullest expression in Egypt. It goes without saying that Pharaoh never makes a mistake, and that his armies are invariably victorious (the Assyrian monarchs too never lost a battle). His athletic prowess is superhuman, and his feats of strength and marksmanship are proudly recorded on monuments. But more than all this, Pharaoh is literally a god incarnate. Even in his lifetime, he is paid divine

---

project. Still, Israel's material accomplishments were far below those of her neighbors, while the religious and ethical teachings of the Bible — as will appear in succeeding chapters — exceed anything produced in these great empires.

honors; after death, he is completely identified with Amon or some other cosmic deity.

It is often said that the Pharaoh Ikh-enaton (about 1380–1362 B. C. E.) was a monotheist. He recognized only the solar disk (Aton) as divine, and his hymn to Aton has an elevation of tone and a moral quality unparalleled in the Egyptian sources. But only the royal family was permitted to worship Aton directly. All others could approach the highest divinity only by worshipping Pharaoh, his earthly regent.

The central event of the Hebrew Bible is the Exodus, the revolt of the Hebrew slaves against Pharaoh, the visible deity. God is not to be identified or allied with an earthly ruler but ranges Himself on the side of the downtrodden. He is the Father of orphans and the Defender of widows (Psalm 68.6). But the God of Israel does not assert His higher authority against alien rulers only. He judges the Israelite kings as well, and they receive His support and approval only so long as they conform to His law of righteousness.

The Mosaic law prescribes that the king shall be chosen by the people, from among "their brethren." The blood in his veins is not bluer than that of his subjects. He must diligently study and faithfully obey the Torah — the revealed law. He must not multiply wives, nor purchase too many horses, nor enlarge his treasury too greatly — lest arrogance should lead him to disregard God's will (Deuteronomy 17). One Biblical writer held the establishment of the monarchy to be itself an act of disloyalty to God, who alone was to be the King of Israel (I Samuel 8). The prophets of Israel indulged in the freest and most outspoken criticism of their kings.

Let us pause here briefly. We possess an Egyptian papyrus known as *The Protests of the Eloquent Peasant*. It tells of a poor farmer victimized by government officials, who voices his complaints against injustice before the Chief Steward, despite threats and flogging. He does not know that Pharaoh has heard about the matter and has commanded the Chief Steward to allow the peasant free expression. In the end, the protestant is vindicated and his just claims are granted.

This interesting document is evidence that there was some regard for human rights in ancient Egypt and that social criticism was not wholly suppressed. But one cannot overlook the caution with which this criticism was voiced. It takes the form of an edifying fiction which does no more than point out the faults of a greedy and corrupt officialdom. There is no attack on the system itself, no suggestion of different or higher standards. Above all, the highest authority is carefully shielded from blame. Pharaoh is divinely wise and altogether good.

For contrast, let us look at some blunt words of a Judean prophet, directed at a reigning monarch who was building a luxurious palace with drafted labor:

"Woe unto him that buildeth his house by un-
    righteousness,
And his chambers by injustice;
That useth his neighbor's service without wages,
And giveth him not his hire;
That saith: 'I will build me a wide house

And spacious chambers,'
And cutteth him out windows,
And it is ceiled with cedar and painted with ver-
  million.
Shalt thou reign, because thou strivest to excel in
  cedar?
Did not thy father eat and drink,
And do justice and righteousness?
Then it was well with him.
He judged the cause of the poor and needy;
Then it was well.
Is not this to know Me? saith the Lord.
But thine eyes and thy heart
Are only for thy covetousness,
And for shedding innocent blood,
And for oppression, and for violence, to do it.
Therefore thus saith the Lord concerning Jehoiakim
  the son of Josiah, king of Judah:
They shall not lament for him:
'Ah my brother!' or: 'Ah sister!'
They shall not lament for him:
'Ah Lord!' or: 'Ah his glory!'
He shall be buried with the burial of an ass,
Drawn and cast forth beyond the gates of Jerusalem"
                              (Jeremiah 22.13–19).

If not downright treason, this was surely *lèse-majesté*.
During a large part of his life, Jeremiah was in trouble.
Several times he barely escaped execution for his bold-
ness. And he was only one of many who courageously
attacked the vested interests.

Jehoiakim, the object of the outburst just quoted,
was a weakling who had little popular support and
held his throne only through the backing of a foreign
overlord. But David, the ablest and most successful

of all the Israelite kings, the darling of his soldiers and the hero of his people, was once denounced to his face by the prophet Nathan — and humbled himself before the rebuke (II Samuel 11, 12). Even the distortions of Hollywood's *David and Bathsheba* cannot completely obscure the grandeur of the prophet's deed.

This independent spirit found its voice chiefly through the prophets but was not limited to them. The vigorous and competent King Ahab once found himself thwarted by a small farmer named Naboth. Ahab wanted to purchase some property from the latter, but Naboth was unwilling to part with the "inheritance of his fathers." The king was angry but apparently felt he could not insist upon the transaction; it was his wife Jezebel, a Phoenician princess, who settled the matter by contriving the judicial murder of Naboth. The property was then forfeited to the crown; but not even Jezebel could prevent the prophet Elijah from speaking out against the infamy (I Kings 21).

Thus, while the other writings of the ancient Near East are a defense of the established order and a glorification of divine or divinely appointed rulers, the Bible subjects both royal and priestly authority to constant scrutiny by the higher tests of righteousness and holiness. The editor of the Book of Kings reviews the lives of all the kings of Israel and Judah, judging them by their fidelity to the Law. He dismisses some of the most successful rulers, whose exploits are mentioned in Assyrian monuments, with the curt remark that they did evil in the sight of the Lord.

It was indeed widely believed that God had chosen

the dynasty of David for everlasting kingship; but the promise was always conditioned by the obedience of the kings to the divine will:

"If (David's) children forsake My law,
And walk not in Mine ordinances;
If they profane My statutes,
And keep not My commandments;
Then will I visit their transgressions with the rod,
And their iniquity with strokes.
But My mercy will I not break off from him,
Nor will I be false to My faithfulness"

(Psalm 89.31–34).

Much of the foregoing exemplifies a general characteristic of the Bible: it reckons with the unpleasant and embarrassing truth. Self-glorification is a common trait of national literatures, ancient and modern; but the Biblical authors deal more severely with their own nation than with any other. (And yet they were not lacking in patriotism).

They recognize frankly that Israel is not the most ancient stock. It does not trace its descent from a god or demigod, nor is it the original tribe from which all other peoples were derived. The first eleven chapters of Genesis sketch the early history of mankind; only at the end of the eleventh chapter do we meet the direct forebears of the Hebrew people. Joshua tells his generation: "Your fathers dwelt of old time beyond the River (Euphrates) — even Terah the father of Abraham and the father of Nahor — and they served other gods" (Joshua 24.2). Nor can Israel lay claim to racial purity: "the Amorite was thy father, and thy mother was a Hittite" (Ezekiel 16.3).

It is a constant element of Biblical thought that God has chosen Israel to be His people in a special sense; but this election does not imply that Israel possessed a necessary and inherent superiority. On the contrary, it sets the shortcomings and sins of the people in sharper relief. The prophets who so bitterly denounced the wealthy and powerful exploiters of the poor did not idealize the proletarian masses. They were equally severe on all who violated God's law, whatever their class or rank. Israel is repeatedly described by Scriptural authors as a stiff-necked people, and its lapses into idolatry are reproachfully recorded. The many disasters that befell the little nation are blamed not on the ruthlessness and cruelty of other powers, but on Israel's own spiritual shortcomings. In their zeal, the prophets sometimes give the impression that their people was morally and religiously inferior to its neighbors. (This was probably not the case: conscientious parents judge other people's children indulgently but are far more exacting with their own).

"Hath a nation changed its gods
  Which yet are no gods?" cries Jeremiah.
  Yet My people hath changed its glory
  For that which doth not profit" (Jeremiah 2.11).

The narrow and bigoted Jonah is contrasted, in the book that bears his name, with heathen sailors who are yet pious and kindly. They know that their ship is in danger because Jonah is a passenger; but they do their utmost to bring the ship back to land before they reluctantly adopt his own suggestion to throw him into the sea (Jonah 1.11 ff.).

As the people is exposed to unsparing criticism, so are its heroes. Not a single character of the Bible is depicted as flawless — not Abraham the friend of God, not Moses the lawgiver. They appear before us in their full humanity, with noble and elevated qualities that rouse our admiration, but with familiar human frailties as well.

An extraordinary manifestation of this Biblical insistence on the whole truth is the constant reminder to the people that they were once slaves in Egypt. Today we think of chattel slavery as a reproach and degradation rather to those who profited by it than to its victims; and perhaps for this reason we no longer feel the full impact of sentences like "thou shalt remember that thou wast a slave in the land of Egypt" (Deuteronomy 5.15). But in an age when slavery was a familiar institution and the slave was juridically less than a human being, it could not have been agreeable to be reminded that one's ancestors had been slaves. Yet this theme constantly recurs in the Bible, not only as a summons to thank the God who redeemed us from this sordid and humiliating status, but also as a challenge to our humanity.

But this subject of slavery must be examined more closely. For it leads us to one of the supreme achievements of Biblical thought: the discovery of mankind.

V

THE DISCOVERY OF
MANKIND

The abolition of chattel slavery has occurred only in recent centuries and has not yet been achieved in all parts of the world; at times, private slave-owning has been replaced by systems even worse, like those of the Soviet Union. It is not surprising therefore that in a period when slavery was completely respectable everywhere, the Bible should have accepted the institution as normal. Many of the Scriptural provisions regarding slaves are comparable to those in other ancient codes. Even the rule that a Hebrew slave must not be kept in perpetual servitude but is to be an indentured servant for no more than six years (Exodus 21.1 ff.) has antecedents in the Near Eastern environment.

But the Torah contains at least three items on this subject that are altogether unique. First, the repeated commandment that slaves as well as freemen shall have the privilege of Sabbath rest.* Such a rule could not exist in civilizations that did not have a Sabbath.

The second provision reads: "If a man smite the eye of his bondman, or the eye of his bondwoman, and destroy it, he shall let him go free for his eye's sake. And if he smite out his bondman's tooth, or his bond-

---

*The English translation in Deut. 5.14 etc. is not sufficiently blunt. "Man-servant" and "maid-servant" are not hired employees, but slaves.

woman's tooth, he shall let him go free for his tooth's sake" (Exodus 21.26–7). The Rabbinic interpreters, no doubt correctly, explain that this law gives freedom to the slave in compensation for any major physical injury inflicted by the master. There seems to be nothing remotely comparable to this law in any ancient code. Not that slaves were invariably abused: sometimes they were, sometimes they were treated kindly. It was not uncommon in ancient times to give a slave his freedom, but such enfranchisement was entirely a voluntary action of the master. To penalize brutality to a slave by freeing the latter, to organize the community to prevent the abuse of a fellow human — this was something new.

Before we consider the third Biblical provision, it is profitable to examine a corresponding section in the Code of Hammurabi:

> "If a seignior has helped either a male slave of the state or a female slave of the state or a male slave of a private citizen or a female slave of a private citizen to escape through the city gate, he shall be put to death. If a seignior has harbored in his house either a fugitive male or female slave belonging to the state or to a private citizen, and has not brought him forth at the summons of the police, that householder shall be put to death" (Hammurabi 16.16; Pritchard, *op. cit.*, p. 166–7).

But the Torah ordains:

> "Thou shalt not deliver unto his master a bondman that is escaped from his master unto thee; he shall dwell with thee, in the midst of thee, in the

place which he shall choose within one of thy gates, where it liketh him best; thou shalt not wrong him" (Deuteronomy 23.16, 17).

These verses were an inspiration to the American abolitionists, even after the Supreme Court, in the Dred Scott decision, repudiated the Biblical law. The Torah presumes that the slave would not have fled from his master and sought sanctuary among us without good reason. It not only forbids us to return him to his owner, but insists that we give him the opportunity for a new start in life.

So radical is this ordinance that scholars have doubted whether it could be carried out in practice and have suggested that it should not be understood literally. But though we find the passage startling, that is no reason to explain it away. There are other laws in the Torah (especially in Deuteronomy) that seem unrealistic and impractical, the expression of a noble purpose rather than the codification of current practice. Perhaps the law of the runaway slave belongs in this category. Still, it is significant that a prophetic spirit in Israel should have dreamed of a social order in which men should no longer be held in bondage against their will.

For the Bible, which sought in the ways we have cited to control slavery and make it less inhumane, proclaims a truth that, carried to its ultimate conclusion, must condemn enslavement as basically wrong. Of many illustrations that we might cite, the words of Job are the plainest and most impassioned:

"If I did despise the cause of my man-servant,
  Or of my maid-servant, when they contended with
  me —
What then shall I do when God riseth up?
And when He remembereth, what shall I answer
  Him?
Did not He that made me in the womb make him?
And did not One fashion us in the womb?"

(Job 31.13–15).

The notion that every one needs and is entitled to
periodic rest from work is so much a part of our
civilization that we take it for granted. But the idea
of the Sabbath is not self-evident. Even as late as the
Roman period, the Jewish Sabbath was disdained as
the outcome of superstition, which led men to fritter
away a seventh part of their life in idleness and (perhaps worse) to reduce in the same measure the produc-
tive power of their slaves and beasts.

Today we see that the Sabbath has inestimable value
for the physical and mental health of the individual,
and even more for his spiritual development. The
Sabbath is a visible affirmation that each person is more
than a cog in the economic machine, that he has a
right to himself — to his own body and to his own
spirit. This is plainly implied in the Biblical legislation
which includes slaves and animals in the commandment
of Sabbath rest (Exodus 20.10, etc.). The development
of the Jewish Sabbath as a day of rest, worship, con-
secration, and family happiness did not occur fully
during the Biblical period. But the essential Sabbath
spirit is well expressed in the prophetic demand:

"If thou turn away thy foot because of the Sabbath,
From pursuing thy business on my holy day;
And call the Sabbath a delight,
And the holy of the Lord honorable;
And shalt honor it, not doing thy wonted ways,
Nor pursuing thy business, nor speaking thereof;
Then shalt thou delight thyself in the Lord"

(Isaiah 58.13–14).

And despite claims sometimes made to the contrary, the Biblical Sabbath is unique. Babylonian sources speak of a day called *Shapatum*, which is etymologically the same as Sabbath; but this Babylonian *Shapatum* was an occasional day of ill omen, on which the activities of certain official personages were restricted. The idea of a weekly rest day for all people came to mankind through the Hebrew Bible.

Indeed, we may say that the writers of the Bible discovered the concept of mankind, and more than that, felt this idea deeply. We have seen it in Job's words regarding his common humanity with his slave. The same outlook appears in references to another group that was underprivileged in ancient times (and sometimes still today) — the foreigners.

Generally, the alien had no rights in the ancient world except insofar as he had obtained the personal protection of a native citizen in the country of his sojourn. Such an institution (what the Romans called *hospitium*) is not clearly mentioned in the Bible. Instead the Torah insists repeatedly that the foreigner be accorded just and humane treatment without specially qualifying for such treatment. "You shall have one statute both for the stranger and for him that is born in the land" (Numbers 9:14 and frequently). But it is not enough to protect the foreigner against injustice. "The stranger that sojourneth with you shall be unto you as the homeborn, and thou shalt love him as thyself; for ye were strangers in the land of Egypt" (Leviticus 19.34).

The picture of mankind as essentially one is carried backward by the Biblical authors to creation and forward to the golden age. The opening chapters of Genesis account for the origin of *man*, not of any segment or branch of humanity. In the Hindu myth, caste distinctions go back to the very beginning: the Brahmins sprang from Brahma's head, the lesser castes from the lower parts of his body. Many peoples have believed that they, or at least their rulers, were direct descendants of a god, and hence of finer material than the rest of mankind. But the Bible sees all men as one stock, created "in the image of God."

It is thus no accident that the Bible is the one ancient writing that projects the vision of a universal human brotherhood, freed from the curse of war, and dwelling together in security and happiness. The closest other peoples came to this was the hope of establishing a world empire in which the conquering nation would maintain order by force. Rome actually approximated this kind of peace by repression. The Biblical ideal is entirely different. World peace is to be achieved not by the use of arms, but by their renunciation:

"They shall beat their swords into plowshares,
And their spears into pruning hooks;

Nation shall not lift up sword against nation,
Neither shall they learn war any more;
But they shall sit every man under his own vine
and under his own fig tree,
And none shall make them afraid"
(Micah 4.3, 4; Isaiah 2).

This is one of the best known and most frequently quoted passages of the Bible; but there is a less familiar paragraph that rises to heights even more sublime. Palestine was the land-bridge between the contending empires of Egypt and Mesopotamia, and the Palestinians suffered horribly through the centuries at the hands of these two rival powers. Yet a prophetic writer envisioned the day when "Israel shall be the third with Egypt and with Assyria, a blessing in the midst of the earth; for that the Lord of hosts hath blessed him, saying: Blessed be Egypt My people, and Assyria the work of My hands, and Israel Mine inheritance" (Isaiah 19:24–25). To gauge the spiritual grandeur of this sentence, we must picture a contemporary democratic Czech saying "Blessed be Germany My people, and Russia the work of My hands, and Czechoslovakia Mine inheritance."

As the Biblical thinkers grasped ever more clearly the vision of universal humanity, they came also to recognize more fully the importance and value of the individual. We speak now not of the glamorous individual, the hero, the conqueror, the demigod. Such exceptional personalities, usually warriors and rulers, are celebrated in the song and story of all peoples. But the average man or woman was simply a part of a larger unit — clan, tribe, or nation — and found whatever significance his life might hold by functioning submissively as part of that unit. It is in the Bible that the importance of the unsensational human being is gradually recognized, in terms of his sensitivities and sufferings rather than of his accomplishments. The Biblical laws stress the importance of delicate consideration for the feelings of the individual. This attitude leads to the emergence of *personal religion*. The Bible does not cease to stress the relationship of the group or nation to deity through the institutions and ceremonies of religion; but more and more it adds to this a recognition of the direct relation of the human heart to God through faith and trust.

VI

THE GOD OF SINAI

We have seen that the Scriptural writings pioneered in proclaiming and championing certain basic human values. The enduring worth of these principles and ideals will be challenged by few modern readers. But when we turn to matters of theology, agreement will not be so quickly achieved, in part at least because of difficulty over the definition of terms. Yet whatever we today may believe or disbelieve about God, we must recognize that the Biblical advance in concept of deity is objectively as great as the advance in ethical and social ideals; and the two elements were always closely related.

The ancient Near Eastern texts teem with names of numberless gods. They detail myths concerning the wars, banquets, loves, and jealousies of these same gods. These deities were not (as was once supposed) completely identified with their images; and yet honors paid to their images constituted an important part of their worship. For all practical purposes, the ancient peoples were idolaters. There was indeed a tendency to rise above mythological polytheism to a broader, more abstract, and more universal concept of deity. There are occasional hints that the different gods of popular religion were only different names for, or different aspects of, one supreme god. But this was a trend that never came to effective expression in practice.

The God of the Bible is the one and only God, Creator of the physical universe, Ruler of all men and nations, Source of all values. He must not be depicted in painting or sculpture, for He is above and beyond all material representation. He has no spouse or female counterpart. His creative acts are never, as so often among other peoples, described in terms of sexual reproduction.

The pagan gods were usually personifications of some aspect of nature — the sky, the sun, the ocean, the Nile, the grain crop. This applies also to the so-called monotheism of Ikh-enaton. He worshipped Aton, described as the sole deity, universal and beneficent, but actually identified with the visible disk of the sun. The God of the Bible, however, is Lord of all nature; He is never confused with any specific natural phenomenon. "The heavens declare the glory of God and the firmament showeth His handiwork" (Psalm 19.1). "Praise the Lord from the earth, ye sea monsters and all deeps, fire and hail, snow and vapor, stormy wind fulfilling His word" (Psalm 148.7–8).

Here is a curious passage from the Egyptian:

"Now Re (the sun god) entered every day at the head of the crew taking his place on the throne of the two horizons. A divine old age had slackened his mouth. He cast his spittle upon the ground and spat it out, fallen upon soil. Isis kneaded it for herself with her hand, together with the earth upon which it was. She built it up into an august snake . . . The august god appeared out of doors, with the gods from the palace accompanying him, so that he might stroll as on every day. The august snake bit him . . . The poison took possession of his flesh."*

There is nothing remotely like this crude myth in the Bible. But there is nothing in all the ancient writings to compare with such affirmations as

"I am the Lord, and there is none else;
I form the light, and create darkness;
I make peace, and create evil;
I am the Lord that doeth all these things"

(Isaiah 45.6–7).

---

*Pritchard, *op. cit.*, pp.16–17.

"To whom then will ye liken Me, that I should be
   equal?
Saith the Holy One.
Lift up your eyes on high, and see:
Who hath created these?
He that bringeth out their host by number,
He calleth them all by name" (Isaiah 40.25–26).

Diligent search will indeed reveal some glimmering
of higher conceptions among the Babylonians and
Egyptians. They certainly believed that the gods had
some concern with righteousness and were the source
of the laws that govern society. Likewise a careful
scrutiny of the Bible will bring to light occasional
mythological references. Some are purely literary:
Milton and Goethe did not believe in the heathen
deities they so often invoked. But it may be granted
that here and there in the Hebrew Bible one can find
survivals of mythical belief, of image worship, of
religious opinions that do not rise to the universal
spiritual level of the selections we have quoted. Nevertheless there is an enormous difference between the
religious writings of Israel and those of her ancient
neighbors. The higher insights of the Egyptian and
Mesopotamian texts are occasional, exceptional, and
fleeting; they had no significant consequences for the
popular cult. But the higher viewpoints of the Bible
are explicit, dominant, and decisive. The cruder notions are for the most part exceptional; they were as
a rule either quietly disregarded or were reinterpreted
in the light of loftier teachings concerning faith and

morality. The ethical monotheism of the Hebrew Bible transformed the life of mankind.

Let us sum up the results of our brief and incomplete inquiry. Ancient Israel was a little people unimportant in numbers, wealth, material culture, military power, political influence. During a large part of its national history it was subordinate to great powers which possessed an advanced technical and artistic civilization. Yet this little people, over a period of centuries, produced writings vibrant with passion and beauty, that proclaim a new and sublime way of life. They taught an unseen, amythical, universal, righteous God. Against the authority of divinely born or ordained kings, they upheld the dignity and freedom of the plain man. They affirmed the unity of mankind, and the right of all men to just and compassionate treatment. They envisioned a world redeemed from tyranny and war, where men might live in harmony and brotherhood under the divine law.

How did they do it? How can we account for this sudden lunge forward? How shall we explain the emergence in this one small people of so many superb religious geniuses and such advanced ethical ideals?

Some students have claimed that Israel borrowed its ideas from other peoples. The claim, as we have seen, is preposterous.

Others have tried to lessen the problem by minimizing the grandeur of the Biblical religion. It is true that we read the Bible today in the light of centuries of interpretation, and may occasionally attach to a particular verse more profound meanings than the original author intended. Nevertheless, to belittle the spiritual greatness of the Biblical seers and scribes is simply to reveal one's own deep-seated prejudice.

Less biased scholars have attempted to explain the development of the Biblical ideas in the light of the social, economic, and political history of Israel. Such researches are profitable beyond question: they help us to understand the Bible better. There are important relationships between the physical and social conditions of a people's life, and its culture and religion.

Yet, though we cannot properly understand the career and the writings of Lincoln without reference to the Civil War background, no amount of research into American social and economic history will account for the sublimities of the Second Inaugural. Still less can the partial reconstruction of certain chapters of ancient history explain the vision and inspiration of Moses, the prophets, and the Psalmists. Simple honesty compels us to admit that our prosaic explanations are lame and insufficient and that we face a profound mystery. And many who have studied and pondered the Biblical words through years of earnest inquiry — without *a priori* theological assumptions — have been led by the Biblical message itself to see here some kind of divine revelation.

But at this point the reader may object: I agree that there are many splendid things in the Bible, but aren't you taking too much for granted when you speak of divine revelation? What about the bloody and brutal pages of the volume? How can you select a few notable utterances that appeal to you, and pass over in silence those that are less attractive?

That is a fair challenge, which we must face seriously.

VII

THE DEFICIENCIES

The contemporary reader of the Bible may encounter some disturbing things in the course of his reading. He may be bewildered or irritated by miraculous tales. Still more troublesome are the episodes where God appears in a personal, quasi-human relation to men, conversing with them, and even permitting them to influence His decisions. The prophetic statements regularly begin with the words "Thus saith the Lord;" sometimes the prophets report in detail the circumstances under which God spoke to them. What are we to make of such claims?

Our difficulties are not confined to a few isolated passages; they involve viewpoints that pervade the entire Bible. It is consistently assumed that the universal Creator has chosen the people of Israel to be His special concern. Can modern man believe such a thing? Or can he accept the notion that a cosmic Deity demands the detailed performance of an elaborate ceremonial cult? This last difficulty is aggravated by the knowledge that parallels to the Biblical rites are found among many other peoples, ancient and modern, and by the realization that many of these observances seem rooted in primitive and even superstitious notions.

Moreover, no great critical acumen is needed to observe many contradictions and discrepancies within the Bible — and not only between the various books, but even within a single chapter.

Still more disturbing than the rational difficulties are the moral ones. Some sections of the Bible breathe a spirit of cruelty. The extermination of the Canaanites is said to have been commanded by God; Israel's failure to carry out this order fully is recorded with reproach. The death penalty is rather freely prescribed, in some cases for ritual violations — though never, be it added, for crimes against property. Polygamy is accepted as legitimate, and the status of women is far from satisfactory to us.

The more sensitive student may also be troubled by the implications of the Biblical doctrine of reward and punishment. Health, prosperity, victory, and contentment are constantly promised as the reward of righteousness and obedience to the Law; wickedness, the Bible endlessly reiterates, will result in personal and national disaster. One asks whether this doctrine of retribution is true and, even more important, whether it is ethically sound. Is there to be no higher motivation for righteousness than the proposition that it pays to be good?

Such difficulties are encountered by the reflective reader of the Bible, but they are not peculiar to our age. Every one of them was pointed out long ago. Certain early Christian heretics were convinced that the Old Testament was not the revelation of the Supreme Deity but the work of a lesser and malignant Power who had temporarily ruled mankind. To bolster this theory, they underscored the real or imaginary moral deficiencies of the Hebrew Bible; their arguments, transmitted through various channels, recur in anti-Biblical writings down to the publications of contemporary "Free-thinkers."

But most of the troublesome passages were pointed out, not by hostile critics, but by devout and reverent students of Scripture. In their detailed and searching study of the holy word, they noted every disturbing item and dealt with it as a challenge to be faced and overcome. Convinced in advance that the Bible is God's revelation, all of it true and divine, their methods and their conclusions were different from those of the modernist. They had no doubt about the authority of the laws, even though some laws seemed incomprehensible to them. It never occurred to them to question the divine inspiration of the prophets. And that God had chosen Israel was to them self-evident.

Yet the ancient and medieval Jewish scholars were often surprisingly bold and "modern" in their outlook. They were fully aware that the Bible is not a single homogeneous product but made up of books composed at different times and under different circumstances. Jewish tradition, in fact, assigned the highest authority to the Torah, the Five Books of Moses; the other Biblical books were deemed a supplement to this primary text.

The Rabbis of the second century had some misgivings about admitting several books to the sacred collection: Ezekiel, because it seemed to contradict the Torah; Proverbs, due to its worldly tone; Ecclesiastes, which contains sentiments verging on the irreligious. These marginal writings were accepted only after they had been satisfactorily interpreted. One teacher held that no such man as Job ever existed, and that the Book of Job is an edifying fiction. Other Rabbis remark on the varied style of different prophetic writers, due to personal traits and to the changing circumstances under which the seers lived.

Jewish teachers did not challenge the miraculous as such; yet they were aware of the uniformity of natural processes. Some of them proposed the theory that at the time of creation God had stipulated that the laws of nature should be suspended on certain future occasions. Thus the marvels by which God dramatically revealed His majesty were somehow integrated into an orderly and reliable universe. Medieval authorities explained the fantastic episode of Balaam's talking ass (Numbers 22), and other passages in which angels appear, as prophetic visions or dreams, not as physical happenings. Jewish philosophers escaped many difficulties by interpreting Biblical expressions as figures of speech or allegories. Though they sometimes took excessive liberties in this regard, they were frequently right: when the Bible speaks of God's "strong hand

and outstretched arm", it is affirming His power, not ascribing physical limbs to Him.

The ancient preachers attempted to rationalize and justify the election of Israel. God, they declared, had offered His Torah to all the peoples of the earth; but none of them was willing to accept its austere moral discipline except the descendants of Abraham.

The rabbis were fully aware of the problem of the ceremonial law. Early in the Christian Era, they divided the commandments of the Law into two categories: First, "those that should have been given if they had not been given" — the ethical commands whose rational basis and social utility is clear; second, "those concerning which Satan (the doubter within oneself) and the Gentiles can raise difficulties." Such precepts, among which they include the dietary laws, are to be regarded as "royal decrees," whose value is precisely in our simple-hearted, unquestioning obedience to them. It makes no difference to God, said a third-century teacher, how we slaughter an animal for food: all such laws were given to discipline *us*.

Maimonides, the twelfth century rationalist, attempted to suggest an inner meaning for each of the ceremonial laws. His interpretation of sacrifice is exceedingly radical. In ancient days, he says, sacrifice was universally practiced. Had God not allowed His people to bring offerings to Him, psychological need would have driven them to sacrifice to the heathen deities. The whole law of sacrifice was thus a concession to the requirements of a certain age.

The moral difficulties pointed out above were relieved

by methods of interpretation that sometimes were so extreme as virtually to abrogate a Biblical law. The principle of "an eye for an eye and a tooth for a tooth" was explained as meaning simply that compensation in money must be paid for physical injuries. (Careful reading of Exodus 21.22–25 suggests that this interpretation may well be the correct one.)

Capital punishment (even for those crimes which we still punish by death) was distasteful to the Talmudic authorities. They therefore introduced so many technicalities into criminal procedure as to make a death sentence virtually impossible.

New legislation, beginning long before the rise of Christianity and continuing far into the Middle Ages, progressively raised the status of woman, until she attained — not full equality, but a large measure of security and dignity. Polygamy was exceptional even during the Biblical period, if only because of economic factors; it was formally outlawed for European Jews by a German Rabbi of the tenth century.

As for the inner discrepancies and contradictions in the Scriptural text, they were pointed out even when they are not obvious at first glance. On the assumption of the essential unity of Scripture, the scholars always found some method of harmonizing the contradictions. At times their methods were artificial and far-fetched, but not a few of the old explanations are worth at least respectful consideration.

In the foregoing pages we have indicated how Jewish teachers of the past dealt with the rational and moral difficulties of the Bible text. Similar procedures were adopted by Christian students of both the Old and New Testaments. Two distinctive features, however, marked Christian interpretation. First, the belief that the Law, though divinely given, was only temporary legislation, and had been abrogated by the death and resurrection of the Christian savior. Second, the conviction that the entire Hebrew Bible, but especially the prophetic writings, foreshadowed the career and teachings of Jesus. This view which assumes that the prophets alluded in some detail to specific events that occurred seven centuries after their time, has now been discarded by many objective Christian scholars.

To sum up: through the centuries, the traditionalists upheld the authenticity, divine origin, and essential unity of Scripture, though they were fully aware of the difficulties involved. Their basic convictions led them to adopt methods of interpretation by which these difficulties were minimized and their position was bolstered. When the change came, it was not due in the first instance to new knowledge — at least, not new knowledge about the Bible — but because of changes in total outlook and philosophy.

To many serious modern students, what is called "Biblical Criticism" — which has sometimes been regarded as an assault on the Bible — is actually a key to the solution of the difficulties we have met in this chapter.

VIII

WHAT IS BIBLICAL CRITICISM?

For many centuries the Bible had been viewed as sacred, authoritative, and infallible. The attack upon this position began in the Western world during the seventeenth and eighteenth centuries. It derived from two main sources. One was the growing scientific temper, with its disposition to question and test inherited beliefs and opinions and its increasing dissatisfaction with supernatural explanations. The second was the advance in methods of linguistic, literary, and historical study, which from the Renaissance onward had been applied to the classic Greek and Roman texts. This second factor was perhaps more decisive than the first. The thinkers of the Middle Ages had been aware of the philosophic difficulties in the Biblical text; but they had found a way out of their trouble by allegorical explanations of Scripture. Thus both the demands of reason and the honor of the Bible were given their due. But when exact literary scholarship made it impossible to wrest the meaning of the Biblical text, the conflict between experimental science and revealed documents could no longer be glossed over. The bolder spirits ceased to accept a statement as true simply because it was recorded in the Bible.

The assault on the authority of Scripture occurred within the Gentile world. During the seventeenth and eighteenth centuries, most Jews were confined in both a physical and spiritual ghetto. Unaware of the new developments in science and philosophy, they adhered calmly to medieval ways of thinking. The chief exception, Baruch Spinoza, was estranged from his Jewish background.

In the light of the new humanistic approach, the difficulties long since noted in the Scriptural text led to far reaching and often startling conclusions. Spinoza frankly based his Biblical researches on suggestions by the medieval Jewish commentator, Abraham ibn Ezra. The latter had cautiously hinted that certain sentences of the Pentateuch must have been written after the time of Moses. But Ibn Ezra implied no more than that there are a few later additions to a Torah which he assuredly believed had been revealed by God through Moses. From the same evidence, Spinoza drew much more radical consequences. He suggested that actually the Torah was compiled some eight centuries after Moses, in the time of Ezra.

And if it is not the work of Moses, its claim to divine authorship and authority must be rejected. Spinoza did not recklessly bandy charges of forgery and fraud, as some of his successors did. He held the Bible to be a work of practical import, intended to inculcate morality and buttress the order of society. But it was not for him an inerrant source of heavenly truth.

Spinoza's methods and conclusions were tempered by his own moderation of spirit and by the sound foundation of Hebraic studies he had received in his boyhood. His followers during the period of the Enlightenment, superficial in knowledge but aggressive in mood, went to extremes in their anti-Biblical utterances. Tom Paine's judgments on the Bible are lively journalism, but not serious scholarship. He was convinced that the biblical books are a series of fabrications, contrived to enslave men's minds, and thus facilitate the enslavement of their bodies. The Book of Job, he admits, is an exception which must have got into the Bible by mistake!

Solid results, however, could not be achieved by hasty guesses, motivated by anti-clerical aims.

Much greater success in the use of the critical method was attained by professional Bible scholars, most of whom stood on a positive though unorthodox theology. Nearly all of them were Protestants; among Jewish pioneers in the field, Abraham Geiger (1810–1874) was one of the first in time and in distinction. The number of Jews participating in the modern study of the Bible has steadily grown; today they are among the most eminent specialists in this field.

This science is often called "Biblical Criticism," an unfortunate term because it seems to imply an attitude of hostility or disapproval. Actually it means no more than the application to the Bible of those exact and critical methods of scholarship that are used in the study of all historical documents. Here we shall not expound at length either the methods or the results obtained, but only suggest their implications for a broad appreciation of the Bible.

Every text copied by hand suffers more or less from

mistakes in transmission. Every scribe makes some inadvertent or intentional changes, omits a word here or adds one there. The more manuscripts of a work we possess, the more complicated is the task of determining exactly what the author wrote. But in this respect the Hebrew Bible is quite different from other ancient writings. For about two thousand years, manuscripts were so carefully scrutinized that all surviving copies are very much alike. Yet even this scrupulously controlled version (the so-called Masoretic text) is not completely uniform. True, most of the manuscript variants are of minor importance; but even these raise for the orthodox believer the question: Which is the authentic word of God?

This rigid supervision of the Hebrew text hardly antedated the Christian era. The Greek translation, made a few centuries earlier, was based on a Hebrew text considerably different from the one we possess. Sometimes its readings make better sense than the present Hebrew version. Moreover, there are passages where both the Hebrew and Greek are unsatisfactory, and plausible emendations (made by conjecture alone) yield better meaning. Some sentences and paragraphs seem to be out of place. Others give the impression of being later insertions. In certain cases scribes appear to have deliberately changed the text for various reasons. The study of these matters constitutes the textual or "lower criticism" of the Bible. Its effect is to undermine the impression of a single, fixed document of revelation.

"Higher criticism" deals with the more interesting

and more hazardous questions of the composition, date, and authorship of the Biblical documents, and with the reconstruction of Israelite history — political and religious — following upon this analysis. The inner contradictions of Scripture are no longer to be explained away: they now serve as evidence of multiple authorship. The Torah and other historical books are generally regarded as composite, made up of documents from different periods, reflecting varied social backgrounds and expressing somewhat different viewpoints. The various sources of the Pentateuch are dated long after the time of Moses; and considerable evidence has been produced to support the guess of Spinoza that the Torah was given its present form about the time of Ezra.

The new scholarship has ascribed a far more decisive and creative role to the prophets, especially the later prophets beginning with Amos. According to the traditional view, the Torah is the basic document; the prophets were simply eloquent preachers who sought to reinforce in their own time the truths revealed through Moses. According to the critical view, the Torah itself has been profoundly influenced by the prophetic insights. The ancient laws and traditions it contains have been considerably recast in the light of the advanced conceptions of the prophets. Some scholars have even held that the prophets were the first to teach a clear ethical monotheism.

In fact, nineteenth-century Biblical criticism went to untenable extremes. It assumed that writing was little known in Israel until the time of David, and that for earlier periods we had only vague traditions, most of them unreliable. The stories of the patriarchs were denied all historical foundation, and the account of Moses and the Exodus was held to contain only the smallest kernel of fact, overlaid with layers upon layers of legend. The history of Israelite religion was interpreted in terms of evolution from a primitive and ritualistic popular cult (not very different from the paganism of other peoples) toward the radical and austere moral doctrine of the prophets; and the final result was said to be a compromise between popular, priestly, and prophetic attitudes.

Later discoveries have necessitated a considerable revision of these views. Archaeology has disposed of the notion that the early Hebrews were illiterate nomads. Writing was common in the most ancient period of Israelite history. Research has also shown that even oral traditions were handed down in the Near East over long periods with surprising accuracy. Scholars today have far greater confidence in the reliability of the Biblical narratives than was the case a generation ago. Even the stories of the patriarchs contain data about geographic and social conditions which rule out the supposition that these narratives are mere legends fabricated centuries after the events they relate.

Some over-zealous fundamentalists have drawn unwarranted conclusions from the conservative trend in Biblical criticism. In no sense do the recent findings of archaeology support the claims of supernatural revelation. What we believe on such a question will be determined by our attitude toward life in general, not by antiquarian studies. The present-day historian may conclude from his researches that the Abraham stories contain some ancient and reliable traditions, without believing that Abraham was ordered by God to sacrifice his son Isaac and that an angel intervened to prevent him from carrying out the command. Few if any competent authorities will deny that some at least of the Hebrew tribes lived in Egypt as an oppressed minority and escaped under the leadership of Moses. But whether Moses could perform miracles by waving his rod is another question altogether.

It would be altogether misleading to say that recent research has discredited Biblical criticism. It has simply corrected some of the mistakes made by earlier scholars on the basis of insufficient source material. There is no field of human knowledge in which old errors are not being corrected and new insights gained.

But critical method has not only broadened our knowledge of the Bible. In addition to the new information it has brought to light, it has also yielded a spiritual gain. It gives us an approach to the Bible which faces the difficulties with intellectual integrity and still retains the great values which the Bible enshrines.

IX

HOW THE CRITICAL
METHOD HELPS

Many an individual who was brought up to regard the Bible as the literal word of God has suffered a bad shock when he re-examined it in the light of modern scientific thought. Unable to believe any longer that the Scriptural writings are of divine origin, he has concluded that they must be fabrication and fraud. (Though even Tom Paine, as we saw, could not resist the magnificence of Job.) The critical approach, however, saves us from so unjust a verdict on one of the choicest possessions of mankind and restores to us the possibility of reading the Bible with appreciation and profit.

It presents the Bible as a body of ancient sources, written and transmitted by men. Composed over a period of about ten centuries, they reflect changing social and cultural conditions and present to us many different minds and personalities. The outlook varies from book to book, and many of the separate books themselves are composite. It is hence no surprise that one consistent doctrine does not emerge from the reading of Scripture. With so many hands contributing, there would have to be discrepancies and disagreements.

We can more readily accept the fact that some passages in the Bible are cryptic, even impossible to translate. We no longer ask: Why should God have made His will so clear in some places, only to baffle us utterly elsewhere? We understand that some Biblical documents are fragmentary and incomplete; that certain passages have been so damaged or corrupted in the course of transmission that they are no longer intelligible; that in other cases, the meaning may be obscured by references to facts or situations which were familiar to the writer's original public but are unknown to us.

We are no longer faced with the hard choice of defending the historical correctness of every Biblical narrative, or dismissing the whole work as imposture. The Book of Jonah, for example, was not composed as part of the "Bible", and we have no reason to assume that the author intended it as sober history. This earnest and profound teacher wished to impress on his readers that God's power extends over all the earth and that His love embraces all His creatures. He cast his teaching in the form of a brilliantly told story which breaks off suddenly when the point has been made clear.

In other books, history and legend are often intertwined; but we can disentangle them with reasonable certainty. Historical data can be recognized not only by internal evidence but by their agreement with the contemporary records of other peoples which archaeology has brought to light. We are aware that even in our sophisticated age, legends grow up around famous and appealing personalities. And though they are not factual, they yet have an importance and value in showing us how the popular mind regarded great men.

Understanding this, we can read with profit the legends that embellish the lives of the Biblical heroes.

Examining the legal sections of the Bible, we reach similar results. Many ordinances reflect the economic, social, and moral conditions of their age. The legal and ethical standards are often different from ours, sometimes we dare say inferior to ours. Frequently (as in the laws about slavery we quoted) we see the Biblical writers striving to modify the traditional pattern in the direction of a more noble and sensitive morality. And some legal sections (for instance, the Jubilee law in Leviticus 25 and the rules of war in Deuteronomy 20–21) were probably never carried out in practice: they project the high ethical vision of ancient idealists.

Sometimes, indeed, theoretical considerations led to just the opposite result. Peaceful scribes indulged on paper in a blood-thirstiness for which they might have had no stomach in real life. One of the most disturbing elements we mentioned previously is the command to exterminate the Canaanites and the condemnation of Israel for not carrying out this injunction fully. Actually the passages in question (as well as some narratives in Joshua which report large massacres) date from long after the time of the conquest of Palestine. No doubt the invasion by the Hebrew tribes was brutal and bloody enough — like all such episodes in history. But it was a piecemeal invasion. Different tribal groups entered the country at different points over a considerable period of time. Many Canaanites were killed, many others driven from the land; but a great many remained and gradually amalgamated with the new-comers.

Later on, the Biblical writers were troubled by the persistence of pagan beliefs and practices in Israel. What was the cause of this evil? They concluded that it was due to the baneful influence of the natives. God must have willed that they be rooted out; the failure of Israel to exterminate the Canaanites was sinful.

The advance in ethical thinking can be studied in regard to a somewhat similar matter. The Phoenician wife of King Ahab made a determined effort to introduce the worship of her god, the Tyrian Baal, into Israel, an effort which the prophet Elijah sturdily fought. Some years later, a general named Jehu overthrew Ahab's successor, killed all the surviving members of the royal family and made himself king. He then extirpated Baal worship by massacre. In this adventure he was supported by the prophets of his day, including the famous Elisha, of whom so many wonderful stories are told. But in the next century, the prophet Hosea recalled the incident with horror. To his mind Jehu had performed, not an act of loyalty to the God of Israel, but a brutal and bloody deed to consolidate his own power. Hosea announced that divine retribution would soon come upon the house of Jehu. (See II Kings 9–10 and Hosea 1.)

The Bible critics of the last generation saw a gradual and steady evolution of the Israelite religion from a primitive tribal cult, in which piety was a matter of group ceremonial, to a universal, spiritual faith centered around an ethic of justice and humanity. More recent research indicates that the process was more complicated and to us more confusing. Evolution did not proceed in a single line. It appears that monotheism was not a late discovery of the great prophets, but was known in the time of Moses. Primitive and advanced concepts, ritualistic and ethical emphases, national pride and broad universalism existed side by side, sometimes in conflict, sometimes in combinations that may seem strange to us.

But whatever the details of the process may have been, the conclusion is much the same. The Bible does not present a single homogeneous doctrine. It is a record of spiritual growth and advance. In any such development there are inconsistencies. The history of American democracy, for example, records periods of progress and of retrogression. It reveals significant sectional differences in regard to social attitudes. And sometimes we are surprised to find that a single individual was progressive in one area of his thinking, and a reactionary on other subjects. Similar phenomena are to be found in the Biblical writings.

Nevertheless, the new approach is helpful and liberating. We realize that had there been no difficulties, no inconsistencies, no moral stumbling-blocks, *that* would have been cause for surprise. How could an ancient compilation of this sort contain only gold and no dross at all? The naive, superstitious, ethically primitive and theologically obsolete elements in the Bible are a kind of guarantee of its authenticity. And they are a means of measuring the achievement of the Biblical seers.

Through the ages men have read the Bible selectively, stressing those items that expressed their own highest insights and ideals, quietly disregarding or re-interpreting passages they found repugnant. We are no longer compelled to distort the plain meaning of Scripture. We can enjoy the miraculous tales, appreciating their penetrating human insights and simple piety, without worrying about the implausible statements they contain. We can pass over the less edifying sections without either trying to justify them or to explain that they do not mean what they appear to say. We are aware that our own advanced culture has aspects which cannot be justified and which we tolerate (to our shame) only because we are accustomed to them; but we know that despite these deficiencies, there are genuine, positive values in our civilization.

The important thing is that the Bible contains, in addition to some materials that are dated, a vast amount that is not only valid for our age, but represents a spiritual level far above our highest attainments. All the more majestic and impressive do the noblest pages of the Bible appear against the background of primitive survivals which Scripture itself records, and against the broader background we have sketched of ancient Near Eastern thought. These pages are unexcelled for their warm humanity, austere morality, social vision, and sublime awareness of God.

We are nearly ready now to approach the basic question of this essay: to state the relevance of the Bible for the modern reader, especially the modern Jew. Only one more task must first be performed.

Since the Bible is not a book, but a collection of writings, we must undertake a brief survey of these writings and their contents.*

X

A SHORT TABLE OF CONTENTS

The Bible has been translated into English many times. The most widely used version, universally regarded as one of the great classics of the English language, is the so called "King James Bible", more correctly the "Authorized Version" of 1611. The magnificent diction of this translation was largely utilized by the group of Jewish scholars who produced the version, published in 1917, that has become standard among English-speaking Jews.** If we compare this American Jewish version with the Authorized Version or any other Bible translation prepared under Christian auspices, we note at once a considerable difference in the order of the Biblical books.

This divergence goes back to the first Bible transla-

---

*Two important general questions were raised at the beginning of Chapter VII: the claim of the prophets to divine inspiration, and the doctrine of the election of Israel. These questions have not been overlooked, but are reserved for the final chapters of this book.

**The Holy Scriptures: A New Translation. Philadelphia, The Jewish Publication Society of America. 1917. (Quotations in this volume are generally taken from the Jewish version.)

tion, the Greek rendering made in Egypt before the Christian era. The Alexandrian Jews who produced this translation arranged the books in an order that seemed to them more correct than the one found in Hebrew manuscripts. This order has been followed by Christian translators, even when their rendering is based on the Hebrew text; but modern Jewish translators have adhered to the arrangement of books in the Hebrew Bible.

The Greek translation, or Septuagint, eventually included a number of Jewish writings not found in the Hebrew Bible. Most of these writings were taken over into the Latin Vulgate, the official Scripture of the Roman Catholic Church. (The Vulgate also contains one interesting work, 4 Esdras, of which both the Hebrew original and the Greek translation have been lost.) The Catholic Old Testament is therefore more extensive than the Jewish Bible or the Protestant Old Testament. The additional books include the two Books of the Maccabees, Tobit, the Wisdom of Solomon, the Wisdom of Ben Sira, and other valuable documents. These writings have often been published separately as the Apocrypha (hidden books).

The Hebrew Bible is divided into three parts: Torah, Prophets, and Writings.

The meaning of Torah has been obscured by the old Greek translators, who rendered it by the word for *law*. For while legal material is an important part of the Torah, it also contains narrative and hortatory sections. A more satisfactory translation might be "revelation" or simply "teaching." Torah means the guidance which God has given man for the conduct of his life. The prophets sometimes refer to their messages as Torah.

In later Jewish usage, the scope of the term was extended. It is applied to this first section of the Bible — the "written Torah" —, more loosely to the Bible as a whole, and then to the "oral Torah," the traditional exposition of Scripture which was eventually crystallized in the vast Talmudic literature.

Tradition ascribed supreme sanctity and authority to the written Torah. The Prophets and Writings had a somewhat lesser holiness, and were to be interpreted in conformity with the Torah.

As we pass in review the various Biblical writings, we shall note one more way in which the Greek translators have exerted influence. Many of the Biblical books are still called by the Greek titles given by these ancient translators, or by names based on the Greek titles. In Hebrew, a number of the books are called simply by their first (or first distinctive) word.

I. Torah (Pentateuch, Five Books of Moses).

1. Genesis ("beginning", Hebrew *Bereshith*) contains the Hebrew traditions concerning the origin of the world, of mankind, and of the people of Israel. It attempts to explain the invention of the arts and crafts, the variety of peoples and languages, the necessity of labor, the existence of sin and death. These ancient tales, which are combined with some very old poetry,

have been strongly influenced in their present form by the advanced religious and ethical concepts of the Biblical teachers. This is strikingly illustrated by the story of the Flood, which is derived from an early Mesopotamian myth. The crude tale of warring gods, who nearly starve when the flood deprives them of sacrificial food, has been completely transformed by the ethical monotheism of Israel.

The stories concerning the beginnings of mankind are followed by the account of the Hebrew patriarchs, from the call of Abraham to the settlement of his descendants in Egypt under the patronage of Joseph. All these graphic and moving stories, according to the findings of critical scholarship, come from sources, which may be classed together as "the prophetic narrative." Mingled with these colorful tales are sections of a more sober cast, which have been ascribed to a priestly source. Sometimes the priestly writing has a noble, if formal dignity, as in the account of creation (Genesis 1); sometimes it manifests a kind of precise repetitiousness, as in the law of circumcision (ch. 17).

2. Exodus (Hebrew *Shemoth*) continues the narrative with the story of the Egyptian bondage, the deliverance under the leadership of Moses, and the giving of the commandments at Mount Sinai. The covenant between God and Israel is violated when the people worship the golden calf, but Moses persuades God to pardon His erring folk. Exodus contains a number of legal sections: laws concerning Passover and Sabbath (chs. 12, 16); the Ten Commandments (ch. 20);

and two organized codes. One of these contains many specific social and ethical ordinances (chs. 21–23); the second is almost entirely ceremonial (34.12–26). There are again a number of priestly sections, including a detailed account of the building of the Tabernacle for sacrificial worship (chs. 25–31 and 35–40).

3. Leviticus (Hebrew *Vayikra*) is derived entirely from the priestly sources. It describes the various types of sacrifices and the occasions when they are to be offered, and treats fully the subject of ritual defilement — from forbidden foods, contact with unclean objects, certain diseases, etc. — and the means of purification from defilement. The priestly writers are also concerned with ethical values. They carefully define the degrees of relationship within which marriage is prohibited, and warn against the crimes of sexual deviation. The great law of holiness (ch. 19) enjoins not only ceremonial precision but the highest and most sensitive standards of moral conduct, climaxed by the "golden rule": "Thou shalt love thy neighbor as thyself" (19.18). Leviticus also contains the idealistic law of the Jubilee, which aimed to establish a kind of economic democracy (ch. 25), and concludes with powerful exhortations concerning the reward of obeying the law and the punishment for disregarding it.

4. Numbers (Hebrew *Bemidbar*). The priestly source supplies dull stretches of statistics regarding a census in the wilderness, and some legislative items; but also the beautiful priestly benediction (6.22–27). Other documents present interesting accounts of Israel's adventures in the desert, especially the fas-

cinating tale of Balaam in which narrative prose is interspersed with lofty poetic rhapsodies (chs. 22–24).

5. Deuteronomy ("second law", Hebrew *Devarim*) is entirely different in tone and style from the rest of the Torah. It is in the form of addresses delivered to Israel by Moses before his death. The first eleven chapters review Israel's deeds and misdeeds in the desert, and voice an eloquent appeal for loyalty to God and His law. This section contains the *Shema*, which has become a kind of Jewish profession of faith: "Hear, O Israel, the Lord our God, the Lord is one" (6.4). The introductory speeches lead to an extensive law code, in which the oratorical style is largely maintained. This code places special stress on the restriction of sacrifice to the one sanctuary "where the Lord shall cause His name to dwell" — presumably the Temple in Jerusalem. Most scholars have therefore connected Deuteronomy with the reformation of King Josiah in 621 B. C. E., when all the local shrines were outlawed (see II Kings 22, 23). The code is an inclusive one, broadly humanitarian in many of its provisions. It is followed by renewed exhortations, two remarkable poems, and the touching story of Moses' death.

II. Prophets (*Nevi'im*).

This section is subdivided into Earlier Prophets and Later Prophets. The books of the Later Prophets are made up chiefly of addresses delivered by the prophets. The Earlier Prophets are actually historical books, in which, however, frequent mention of the prophets and their activity is made. These historical books present a fairly connected (though by no means complete) history from the invasion of Canaan to the destruction of the independent commonwealth in 586 B. C. E.

The Book of Joshua is apparently derived from the same sources as the Pentateuch. The other books in this series consist of various early documents (whose sources are sometimes mentioned by name) joined together by a moralizing framework which in viewpoint and style is strongly reminiscent of Deuteronomy.

1. Joshua relates the conquest and division of the land.

2. Judges (*Shofetim*) deals with the period of disorganization and tribal struggle between the conquest and the establishment of a strong national state. The so-called "judges" were in fact tribal chieftains.

3. Samuel has been divided into two books because of its length (so also Kings). In this work the role of the prophets comes to the fore. We read of the prophet Samuel's struggle to unify the people and free them from the overlordship of the Philistines; of Saul's ill-starred attempt to rule; and of the rise and triumph of David. The chronicle of David's reign is a masterpiece of vivid and unflatteringly honest historical writing. The book contains several poetic selections, some at least the work of David himself.

4. The two books of Kings extend from the accession of Solomon to the destruction of Jerusalem. The editor gives much space to the building of Solomon's temple, and in the spirit of Deuteronomy stresses the

law of the single sanctuary. Scattered through a rather sober chronicle are stories of prophets — notably Elijah, Elisha, and Micaiah. In addition to many miraculous episodes these stories contain much of moving human content and high moral purpose.

Each of the books of the Later Prophets bears the name of an individual. We have already characterized the Book of Jonah;* the rest of the books consist chiefly of utterances by the prophets, as they were written down or dictated after their public delivery. Occasionally these books present biographical or auto-biographical material, or excerpts bearing on the history of their time.

Concerning many prophets we know nothing except their names; and in some cases, we do not even know their names. For scholars agree that some of the prophetic works are compilations, and that the author whose name they bear is not the only contributor. The most important instance is the book of Isaiah.

The prophet Isaiah son of Amoz lived in the eighth century B.C.E. To him scholars ascribe a large part (not all) of the first thirty-nine chapters of his book. Chapters 40 through 55 are the work of an unknown seer who lived two centuries later during the Babylonian Exile. He is often referred to as Second Isaiah (Deutero-Isaiah).** The final chapters may be still later, and are frequently designated Trito-Isaiah.

---

*Above, p. 51.

**The first Bible student to distinguish between the two parts of the Book of Isaiah seems to have been Moses ibn Gikatilla, a Spanish Jewish commentator of the eleventh century.

The prophetic books are not in chronological order. They are arranged as three "major" and twelve "minor" prophets. The terms major and minor, used in their Latin meaning, refer to the size of the books, not their relative importance. (In Jewish tradition, the "minor" prophets are called simply "The Twelve.")

The following table indicates the approximate chronological order of the prophetic writings. The numerals indicate the order of the Hebrew Bible.

6. Amos 4. Hosea 1. Isaiah 9. Micah	} 8th century B.C.E.	
10. Nahum 12. Zephaniah 11. Habakkuk 2. Jeremiah	} 7th century	} Pre-Exilic
3. Ezekiel (1. Deutero-Isaiah)	} 6th century	} Exilic
13. Haggai 14. Zechariah	} 5th century	} Post-Exilic
7. Obadiah 5. Joel 15. Malachi	} uncertain	

8. The Book of Jonah is probably a post-exilic composition; but its hero was a historical figure of the eighth century (II Kings 14.25).

The chief theme of the pre-exilic prophets was the imminent doom of the nation — a doom merited by unrighteousness in government, social injustice, and personal immorality, as well as by defection to paganism. As they point out the moral failure of the nation, the prophets affirm magnificent standards of individual and social righteousness. They insist that the essential element in religion is ethical, not ceremonial; and they severely attack the sacrificial cult which was central in the religion of their contemporaries. (According to tradition, the prophets objected not to sacrifice as such, but to sacrifice without righteousness; and this interpretation is still maintained by many modern scholars.)

Though all the prophets foretell the impending destruction of Israel, a note of ultimate hope soon makes its appearance. From Hosea onward, the prophets suggest that the punishment, though it must be tragically severe, will not obliterate the people altogether. The downfall will have a chastening effect at least on a saving remnant, whom God will at last restore to create an ideal commonwealth.

Jeremiah and Ezekiel lived through the destruction of the state of Judah. Prophets of doom in the days when the people still hoped for deliverance, they began to offer messages of encouragement precisely when the situation became desperate. Actually they had not changed their fundamental affirmation — that God's will is fulfilled in human history. The same righteous God who must punish the sinful nation will discipline and regenerate their spirits, and so help them to be worthy of redemption and restoration. This leads to a broader vision of the reconciliation of all mankind in peace under God.

Ezekiel differed from the other prophets in the high importance he attached to the Temple cult and to ritual precision, though he also stressed moral values. He was not as sublime a poet as his fellow-prophets, but produced many pages of vivid and dramatic prose. A little later the Second Isaiah delivered glowing messages of hope, in which the universal rule and love of God and the vision of a redeemed humanity reach their climactic expression. The latter chapters of Isaiah have always been the best loved and most widely read portion of prophetic literature.

The post-exilic prophets delivered messages both of hope and of rebuke, according to the circumstances under which they spoke. Upholding firmly the social idealism of the earlier seers, they were yet for the most part champions of the Temple and its sacrificial worship. In some of the latest prophets we note a tendency toward a new type of vision, called "apocalypse" — in which the secrets of the "end of days" are revealed (see below, the Book of Daniel).

III. Writings (Hagiographa, *Kethuvim*).

1. Psalms (*Tehilim*): This is undoubtedly the world's most important collection of religious poetry. Many of the lyrics were composed for use as hymns, to be sung by the Temple choir or by the people

(95, 136). Others are outpourings of intensely personal feeling (73, 139). But frequently the Psalmist, though he speaks in the first person singular, is voicing the needs and yearnings of the entire nation (for example, Psalm 9/10, which was originally one poem, and Psalm 66). These poems run the whole gamut of human emotion, from self-abasement and despair to tranquil faith and exultant thanksgiving. A few are more reflective than lyrical, notably Psalm 119, a compendium of pious thoughts arranged in alphabetical order.

2. Proverbs (*Mishle*): This collection of wise sayings, mostly brief, is not dissimilar to the wisdom literature of other oriental peoples. The section beginning at 22.17 is so similar to an Egyptian papyrus that there must be some connection between the two. Much of the advice contained in Proverbs is practical, worldly, and expedient; but this prevailing mood is modified by many utterances that strike a more characteristically Jewish note of piety and social responsibility.

3. Job is a dramatic treatment of the problem of evil and suffering in the world, in the form of a poetic dialogue with a narrative introduction and conclusion. Job, a model of rectitude and piety, is overwhelmed by misfortunes. His friends infer that he is suffering punishment for prior sins, but Job maintains his innocence, even against God. At length God appears and vindicates Job as against his friends; but the existence of evil remains a mystery. The second part of the book has suffered from damage and from in-

sertions into the text, and is often hard to understand; but the work as a whole remains one of the most deeply felt and magnificently written expressions of the tragic spirit.

4. Song of Songs (*Shir HaShirim*), a collection of impassioned love-lyrics. For generations this booklet was explained as an allegory of God's love for Israel; but it seems plain that these beautiful poems celebrate the simple love of men and women. They were perhaps intended for singing at marriage feasts.

5. Ruth: A tender story of a Moabite woman, who after the death of her Judean husband remained faithful to his family and religion. By alleging that King David was descended from Ruth, the author may have been protesting against certain chauvinistic and anti-alien trends in his own time.

6. Lamentations (*Echah*) consists of five doleful poems, bewailing the downfall of Jerusalem and praying for her restoration. The tradition that ascribes them to Jeremiah is probably unfounded. The poems are genuinely pathetic, but lack spontaneity; all but one are written in a somewhat artificial form.

7. Ecclesiastes ("The Preacher," *Koheleth*): This fascinating and in many ways baffling book is made up largely of dour and pessimistic reflections on the vanity of human efforts. Its predominantly skeptical comments are interspersed with practical observations in the style of the old "wisdom", and with occasional affirmations of a more positive religious character. These shifting viewpoints have been variously explained.

8. Esther: This exciting narrative tells how the Jews of Persia were saved from extermination by the courage of Esther, the consort of the Persian king, and how the Purim festival was established to celebrate the happy deliverance. Though many scholars have defended the account as entirely (or at least, partly) historical, their arguments are open to serious doubt. It is hardly accidental that the author — as if to avoid offence — has consistently avoided using the name of God and kept his story altogether secular. Characteristically, even pious Jews have tolerated humorous versions of the Purim story, though they would have been shocked at burlesquing any other portion of the Bible. The Greek version of Esther contains extensive additions which give it a more serious religious tone.

9. Daniel is classified among the prophets in Christian, but not in Jewish editions of the Bible. The first part contains tales about heroes who were true to their faith despite persecution, and were miraculously saved from death. The second is made up of cryptic visions, and is the chief Biblical example of the literary form called apocalypse. (We possess many extra-Biblical examples.) In these writings, an ancient hero is made to predict the future sufferings of the people and their eventual deliverance at God's hands. While Daniel is supposed to have lived during the Babylonian exile, the book was almost certainly written between 168 and 165 B.C.E. During these years the Syrian overlord of Palestine was attempting to force upon the Jews the worship of Zeus; the book was written to

inspire the people to be faithful despite persecution. Portions of Daniel are written in Aramaic, a language cognate to Hebrew, which gradually replaced the latter as the spoken tongue of Palestine.

10. Ezra, 11. Nehemiah, and 12. Chronicles (*Divre Hayamim*) were originally one book, of which Chronicles was the first part. It is a summary of Biblical history from creation to the end of the Babylonian exile. Up to the accession of David, the material is presented chiefly in genealogical form. The main body of the work traverses the same material as II Samuel and the Books of Kings, but omits much that is found in these books while adding new material. The Chronicler was particularly interested in the Temple service and priesthood.

Ezra and Nehemiah contain a fragmentary account of the reorganization of Jewish life in Palestine after the Exile. The books contain excerpts from the memoirs of Ezra, an authority on the Torah and a leader of religious reforms, and from those of Nehemiah, an influential Persian official who was also a devout and loyal Jew.

Note: Proverbs, Job, and Ecclesiastes are often classified together (along with the apocryphal Wisdom of Solomon and Ben Sira) as "the wisdom literature," though actually they are very different from each other in spirit.

Song of Songs, Ruth, Lamentations, Ecclesiastes, and Esther are referred to as the Five Scrolls (*Megilloth*), and each is associated with a particular occasion in the Jewish religious calendar.

XI

WAY OF LIFE

Our brief survey makes plain both the variety and the incompleteness of Biblical literature. Goethe's phrase, "fragments of a great confession," has been well applied to the Hebrew Scriptures. These writings do not offer either a continuous and well organized history or a systematic philosophy. The legal sections too, though extensive, are incomplete; in order to live by them, the Jewish people soon found it necessary to supplement them by free interpretation and by unwritten traditions.

But perhaps this incompleteness is a chief source of the Bible's power. Philosophic systems are among the most perishable of goods. The Bible offers us something different: insights, suggestions. It opens doors. It challenges us to find the way. Above all, it is concerned with the actual experiences and problems of human beings.

The philosopher Spinoza, whose outlook was pagan though his origins were Jewish, chose to contemplate experience "under the aspect of eternity." Thus the infinite variety of life was reduced to a series of abstractions, expressed in quasi-mathematical form. The Biblical method is the exact opposite. It presents "eternal values" — the intuitions of faith and righteousness — in terms of specific and concrete situations.

For example, there is a great deal in the Bible on the subject of justice, but there is nothing like the

Platonic enterprise of defining justice in such broad terms as will apply to every situation. Instead, the Torah legislates for a case in which A's ox gores B's ox, or in which property entrusted by A to B has been damaged by B's negligence, and declares the just method of settling the claims involved. Or from a prophet's stinging condemnation of those who sell grain unfit for food and give short measure at that (Amos 8.5, 6), we readily infer his notions of what social justice demands. Issues of justice arise in vividly told narratives (II Samuel 12, I Kings 3, Jeremiah 26). In every instance, the treatment is the reverse of academic. It is both concrete and passionate:

> "How long will ye judge unjustly,
> And respect the persons of the wicked?
> Judge the poor and fatherless;
> Do justice to the afflicted and destitute.
> Rescue the poor and needy;
> Deliver them out of the hand of the wicked"
>
> (Psalm 82.2–4).

The events to which the Biblical writers refer occurred long ago; the situations may be quite different from those of our own time; and yet the intense concern over right and wrong gives the ancient documents a continuing vitality and makes us feel that their message is addressed to our generation.

Not every word of the Bible has a contemporary ring for every reader at every time. It has been well said that each age has its own Bible. Many an interpreter of the sacred writ has in fact read his own notions into the text and completely obscured its real meaning. But even if we avoid such procedures and allow the Bible to speak to us in its own terms, our ability to absorb and react will vary according to personal differences and to changing circumstances. Yet we dare not hastily decide that because a portion of Scripture seems to have no message for us, it is permanently outmoded and obsolete. A personal experience may clarify this remark.

The prophet Nahum has always been a relatively neglected writer. His short book celebrates the downfall of the Assyrian Empire and the destruction of the capital city of Nineveh. Unlike his contemporaries, who castigated the shortcomings of their own people, Nahum exulted over the collapse of Judah's great enemy. Modern critics, while admitting his literary genius, have been inclined to classify Nahum as one of the "false" prophets denounced by Jeremiah for nurturing the national pride instead of rousing the national conscience.

Yet the present writer happened to study the Book of Nahum shortly after the fall of France in World War II and was startled by sentences that seemed intended for Paris, "*la ville lumière*," who had "multiplied her merchants above the stars of heaven" (Nahum 3.16).

"Watch the ways," says the prophet, "make thy loins strong,
Fortify thy power mightily . .
The shield of his mighty men is made red,
The valiant men are in scarlet,
The chariots are fire of steel in the day of preparation,

And the cypress spears are made to quiver,
The chariots rush madly in the streets,
They jostle one another in the broad places,
The appearance of them is like torches,
They run to and fro like lightnings" (2.2, 4, 5).

But the military preparations are vitiated by the
breakdown of morale among a people that has lost its
vision and idealism:

"All thy fortresses shall be like fig-trees with the
first-ripe figs;
If they be shaken, they fall into the mouth of the
eater.
Behold, thy people in the midst of thee are women;
The gates of thy land are set wide open unto thine
enemies" (3.12, 13).

And these cogent words are from one of the lesser
books of Scripture!

And so, at long last, we come to the direct question:
what is the importance of the Bible for the modern
man, above all for the modern Jew? We have found
important answers, which are still not *the* answer:
The Bible is intensely interesting. It is a collection of
literary masterpieces. It is indispensable for the understanding of Western culture. It supplies the Jew with
the means of comprehending himself in terms of his
own background. But over and above all this, the Bible
is the book of today, the book that speaks to every
generation.

A man comes to mind, a successful professional man,
American born and educated, with only a modest
training in matters Jewish. Out of the blue he was

struck by tragedy, the sudden death of a beloved daughter. And when his friends gathered to express their sympathy, he sat down with them and read to them from the Book of Job.

What has the Bible to say to us?

Many things, according to our needs, our situation, our willingness to accept and our power to absorb. It has little to offer those who do not view life seriously and are concerned only with maintaining a hard enameled surface to conceal the emptiness or weakness underneath. Even for them, the cynical Ecclesiastes may supply the needed thought: for clearly his counsel that "it is comely to eat and to drink and to enjoy pleasure" is a counsel of despair, and its conclusion is "vanity of vanities."

But those who regard life as a challenge and high opportunity find the Bible a lamp unto their feet and a light unto their path.

For the Bible is not a book of static dogma or timeless contemplation. It points to a road that leads forward and upward. It is a summons to a task. It has often been said, but it is of the essence and must be repeated: for the Biblical writers, the golden age is not in the past, not in the lost Eden, but in a future yet to be realized. The drama of history, which began with the creation of man, reaches its culmination only in the messianic age to come. How this fulfillment is to be achieved is a mystery, as life itself is a mystery. The Biblical writers are not too proud of their humanity to hope and seek for divine grace. They cherish the promise that God will take the stony heart from us and give us a heart of flesh, will make us more worthy of His forgiving and reconciling love (Ezekiel 36.26).

Yet it is equally clear to them that man cannot accept his own faults complacently and with folded hands wait for God to forgive him because "*c'est Son métier*." Man's moral striving, his own effort to achieve personal righteousness and to build the righteous society, is somehow integral and indispensable to the final consummation. "Return unto Me, and I will return unto you" (Malachi 3.7). These words of the prophet are correctly explained by a Rabbinic parable of the king's son who wanders away from home and despairs of his ability to find his way back. "Come back as far as you can," runs his father's message, "and I will come to meet you the rest of the way."

The Bible is the book of life in this world. Through most of Scripture, the concept of a future life is vague and shadowy, and some writers seem to reject it altogether. Only in the latest documents of the Bible is there an unequivocal affirmation of blessed immortality. The Hebrew Bible, then, does not negate the hope of a life beyond this one, but it does not set the attainment of heavenly bliss as the primary aim of human behavior or of religious striving. The center of attention is occupied by the righteous deed.

Perhaps the stress on this world may account for the somewhat rigid and materialistic system of rewards and punishments set forth in several Biblical books, the view to which the author of Job took such vehement exception. This concept of retribution cannot, however, be too lightly dismissed. It often pays to be good, and honesty is frequently the best policy. The reverse is likewise true in many instances. The rule holds good particularly of large groups. National stability and prosperity depend on the maintenance of moral and spiritual values. This is the consistent message of the prophets, and it seems to be thoroughly documented by the historians from Thucydides to Toynbee. The theory breaks down only when we suppose it to be a mechanical and invariable rule, so that every misfortune is regarded as the consequence of sin and every stroke of good luck is an inducement to self-righteousness. Very frequently the Bible upholds the thesis — which most of us still live by — "Be good in order to be happy." But the loftiest utterances of Scripture maintain a far higher morality: "Ye shall be holy; for I the Lord your God am holy." (Lev. 19.2). The sense of communion with God is the true reward of righteousness (see Psalm 73, end).

And this holiness does not require withdrawal from contact with a sinful world. Even in ritual matters, it was anticipated that defilement would occur, and means of purification were provided. As for morality, the avoidance of sin by monastic segregation from the realities of daily work and social intercourse was not even considered.

It is assumed that all men will do wrong, not because of a fatalistic "original sin," but because human beings do not always live up to their own highest possibilities. Sinfulness is an unmistakable fact. The Biblical authors do not indulge in rosy illusions about man's goodness, nor dismiss his wrongdoings as mere peccadilloes or psychological deviations. But there is a double corrective of sin. On the one hand, there is the constantly repeated assurance that God is merciful and gracious, full of compassion and ready to forgive. On the other hand, man has the opportunity and capacity to return to God. This emphasis on return ("repentance" is an inadequate translation) is the root of Biblical optimism. Return to God implies a return to His law: a change of heart that shows itself in conduct. The sin-offerings prescribed in the priestly law were not a substitute for moral regeneration and could in fact be sacrificed only after the penitent had confessed his fault and made whatever restitution was possible.

The fact that the ethical teachings of the Bible are presented in the form of specific legislation, of ancient narrative, or of prophetic criticism of situations long since past, might (one supposes) make the Biblical message seem obsolete. Why should I be concerned if an oriental potentate had one of his soldiers liquidated so that he could add the soldier's wife to his harem? In this age of mechanized agriculture, what interest can I have in the rule that an ox must not be muzzled while he tramples the grain to thresh it (Deuteronomy 25.4)? What personal involvement can I have in prophetic attacks on a society where chattel slavery and absolute monarchy prevailed?

But the modern reader reacts none the less to such passages. The Biblical writers were so alive, and their concern with the situations mentioned was so intense, that their words continue to throb with vitality. An academic treatise on ethics but recently off the press may yet seem more remote from our life than the story of David and Bathsheba, the Deuteronomist's requirement of kindness to animals, or the flaming indignation of Amos against those who would sell the poor for silver and the needy for a pair of shoes.

The relative simplicity of the Biblical civilization enables us to grasp its central values more readily. In our complex and interdependent world, the determination of right and wrong in a given situation may involve the balancing of many conflicting factors and the correct interpretation of highly technical data. It is all the more necessary, therefore, for us to maintain an awareness of the basic, "raw" distinctions between good and bad, human and inhuman, which the Bible provides.

We read, for example: "When thou dost lend thy neighbor any manner of loan, thou shalt not go into his house to fetch his pledge. Thou shalt stand outside, and the man to whom thou dost lend shall bring forth the pledge outside to thee" (Deuteronomy 24.10, 11). We can understand this with a minimum of commentary. The poor man may have to pawn one of his possessions to secure a needed loan; but he can be spared the humiliation of standing by while the creditor inspects his few pitiful belongings to see which he will keep as a pledge. This sensitive awareness of human feelings, this concern for the worth of individual personality, has to be translated by us into terms of modern living. But the clear statement and vivid illustration of the imperative is invaluable.

In the Bible, personal character and social righteousness interpenetrate and combine to form a single ethical demand. Our modern world has lost much by distinguishing too sharply between these elements. The "evangelical" approach, which sought to rouse the conscience of individuals and to elevate personal character, has been ineffective in dealing with economic or political injustices which no amount of personal high-mindedness could rectify. A number of good individuals do not necessarily add up to a good society. The collective approach, on the other hand, associated especially but not exclusively with Marxism, assumes without proof that a juster system of distributing wealth or administering laws will produce better and happier people. The Bible, without detailed analysis, demands both personal and group righteousness.

Though it constantly reflects the wonder and beauty of the natural world, Scripture avoids the pagan deification of nature and the equally pagan interpretation of man as part of nature. "The heavens declare the glory of God" (Psalm 19.1); but God is the Lord of nature, not merely its indwelling Spirit.

> "He stretcheth out the north over empty space
> And hangeth the earth over nothing.
> He bindeth up the waters in His thick clouds;
> And the cloud is not rent under them . . .
> Lo, these are but the outskirts of His ways;
> And how small a whisper is heard of Him!
> But the thunder of His mighty deeds who can
> understand?" (Job 26.7, 8, 14).

As God is distinct from nature, so man is distinct from both God and nature. Though he is created "in the image of God" (Genesis 1.26), there is yet an immeasurable gulf between Creator and creature.

"When I consider the heavens, the work of Thy
   fingers,
The moon and the stars which Thou hast estab-
   lished,
What is man, that Thou art mindful of him
And the son of man, that Thou thinkest of him!"
                              (Psalm 8.4, 5).

But — and this is essential — God does consider
man, and has given him a status and dignity different
from that of the rest of creation. And this distinction
is a fact, despite the genetic relationship of man to
the other primates.

"Yet Thou hast made him but little lower than the
   angels,
And hast crowned him with glory and honor.
Thou hast made him to have dominion over the
   works of Thy hands,
Thou hast put all things under his feet" (vv. 6, 7).

The Bible recognizes man's inherent difference from
other creatures; it does not belittle man cynically,
nor does it sentimentally idealize him. Its writers
display an almost flawless insight into human behavior
and motive. This is revealed, without sophisticated
analysis of nuances in the Proustian manner, by an
intuitive grasp of the way people act and talk. The
insights appear in colorful narrative, in the shrewd
comments of Proverbs and Ecclesiastes, and in the
searching criticisms of the prophets.

The Psalms, on the other hand, express all the
moods of human emotion. That is why, through the
ages, the Psalter has provided men and women with

words for what they themselves felt but could not articulate. Here are poems of springtime delight in the world and in life, of tranquil confidence, of courage amid adversity. Here, too, are the pathetic notes of disappointment, fear, and loneliness, and the unrestrained tones of tragic despair. Yet even the most agonized cries, mounting bitterly and angrily to God, imply some ultimate hope:

"Awake, why sleepest Thou, O Lord?
Cast not off forever.
Wherefore hidest Thou Thy face,
And forgettest our affliction and our oppression?"
(Psalm, 44.24, 25).

The future is never written off, even in the darkest moments; and elsewhere, the assurance of something better ahead glows with messianic splendor. And though, as we have seen, the chief emphasis of the Bible is on this world, the hope of blessed immortality is not overlooked:

"Many of them that sleep in the dust of the earth shall awake ... And they that are wise shall shine as the brightness of the firmament; and they that turn many to righteousness as the stars for ever and ever" (Daniel 12.2, 3).

The Biblical writers, when hard pressed, are not abashed to confront God himself with their insistent demands. This has been referred to as the "Promethean element" in Scripture, but the term must not be taken too strictly. Prometheus condemns Zeus as a wicked tyrant; helpless, he considers himself superior to the mighty god. But the Biblical protestants appeal from God to Himself. "Shall not the Judge of all the earth do justly?" exclaims Abraham (Genesis 18.25). Job complains similarly "Is it good unto Thee that Thou shouldest oppress, that Thou shouldest despise the work of Thy hands?" (10.3). The Bible plumbs the physical and moral evils of our existence to the depth, and refuses to distort the facts even for God's benefit; yet it insists that the paradox must have a resolution, and will not let the last word be a word of total defeat.

For a one-sided obsession with evil such as darkens the sky in our thermonuclear age is just as unrealistic as a saccharine optimism. Within the same book of Psalms we read

"I am afflicted and at the point of death from my
        youth up;
I have borne Thy terrors, I am distracted.
Thy fierce wrath is gone over me;
Thy terrors have cut me off"

and also

"Let the sea roar, and the fulness thereof,
The world and they that dwell therein,
Let the floods clap their hands,
Let the mountains sing for joy together,
Before the Lord."

                        (See Psalm 88.16, 17, and 98.7–9).

XII

IS THE BIBLE THE
WORD OF GOD?

We have offered an answer to the central question with which we started. The chief value of the Bible is not in its literary power, its pervasive influence on Western culture, or its usefulness for Jewish self-comprehension. For the Bible has relevant things to say to the contemporary reader. Its profound insight into human behavior, its unfailing concern for human needs, its exacting morality, its insistence on a righteous social order, its vision of the reconciliation of mankind in brotherhood and peace, its tremendous intuitions about man, the world, and God, its sublime poems of worship and aspiration — all these speak to us with a force we cannot disregard. These values are in no way lessened because they appear in ancient documents which contain also materials of lesser interest and sometimes express viewpoints which we cannot in honesty and good conscience accept. For the obsolete (or seemingly obsolete) elements in the Bible are likewise useful in their own way for our instruction.

But granting the importance of the Bible, we may still ask: what about its "inspiration"? At the start of our inquiry, we put aside the assumption that the Bible reached us through a supernatural process and that it possesses inherent divine authority. But now that we have examined its contents, can we in any sense call it the word of God? The question is the more difficult and necessary because the claim of divine inspiration was not merely made on behalf of the Bible: this claim appears many times in Scripture itself.

The great literary prophets in particular pose this problem in a form that cannot be evaded. For the most skeptical of critics agrees that we possess the actual words that the prophets dictated or wrote down; and they introduced their utterances with "Thus saith the Lord." What are we to make of this?

"Freethinkers" have accused the prophets of deliberately deceiving their listeners. A less hostile suggestion is that Moses and the prophets devised the benevolent fiction of divine inspiration in order to commend wholesome physical or moral practices to the people. Such suggestions cannot be seriously considered. Any one who reads the prophets without initial prejudice must sense their passionate sincerity. The luckier prophets had to endure contempt and abuse; some paid for their outspokenness with their lives. When the prophets declared that God spoke to them, they meant it.

Then, if they were honest, were they normal and sane?

Present-day ministers are not infrequently visited by persons who make similar claims to have received divine revelations. But among those who have favored the present writer with accounts of their visions, not one brought him a message of recognizable content. Such individuals are immersed in incoherent fantasy and have almost lost contact with familiar reality They must be judged as unfortunate psychopaths, not only on clinical grounds, but also for theological reasons. God certainly has no need to "reveal" such empty vaporings!

Even in ancient times, some skeptics asserted that the "prophet is a fool, the man of spirit is mad" (Hosea 9.7). And in our psychologically oriented generation, scholars have not overlooked the emotional tensions and the sometimes fantastic imagery of the prophetic oracles. The attempt has been made, for instance, to explain Ezekiel's conduct in psychiatric terms. This is a most hazardous undertaking. Some of the experiences Ezekiel reports may seem to us pathological: loss of consciousness, compulsive acts, grotesque visions. But such phenomena were not unusual among the professional prophets with whom Ezekiel had some affinity; he may have had ecstatic trances because he expected to and because it was expected of him. Certain it is that Ezekiel — in whom these peculiar phenomena are more marked than in any other literary prophet — presented his message in a particularly systematic, logical, and argumentative form. Even his most fantastic visions contain a coherent and readily interpreted symbolism. One wonders at times whether they were not contrived rather than spontaneous.

But let us turn to another prophet who presents the issue more simply. Jeremiah exclaims:

"O Lord, Thou hast enticed me, and I was enticed,
Thou hast overcome me, and hast prevailed;
I am become a laughing-stock all the day,
Everyone mocketh me.
For as often as I speak, I cry out,
I cry: 'Violence and spoil';
Because the word of the Lord is made
A reproach unto me, and a derision, all the day.
And if I say: 'I will not make mention of Him,
Nor speak any more in His name',
Then there is in my heart as it were a burning fire
Shut up in my bones,
And I weary myself to hold it in,
But cannot" (Jeremiah 20.7–9).

It is too easy to dismiss this as "compulsive." What is the nature of the compulsion? It is the moral imperative to proclaim an unwelcome truth and to incur the resentment of those who hear it. It is the irresistible call of that duty which Wordsworth called "stern Daughter of the voice of God." There is nothing irrational about it. Jeremiah's words throb with anguish, but they are completely lucid in thought and chiseled in expression. Jeremiah is convinced that this overpowering inner urge to do the right to his own hurt is literally the voice of God.

Few of the prophets allow themselves such intimate, subjective outpourings as Jeremiah. But their utterances are regularly characterized by the combination of white-hot intensity with well-ordered clarity.

Wherever the prophetic message is obscure to us, it is almost certainly because of an allusion to some circumstances of which we are not informed, or else because of damage to the original Hebrew text. The prophets were not rationalists, yet their thinking and style was exceedingly rational. Their prophecies are poetic in substance and structure, sometimes even elegant, yet free from artifice and embellishment. Their arguments are cogent and effective. Though they never stooped to conciliate their hearers, they were skillful in attracting an audience by dramatic object-lessons or provocative opening sentences. Their insight into the springs of human behavior, and into the national and international affairs of their own time approaches the uncanny.

Amos was a shepherd from the barren uplands of Judah who almost certainly could not read and write. Yet in a time of apparent national strength and prosperity he foresaw the collapse that was bound to occur when the Assyrian military machine moved westward — a catastrophe that did not occur until a generation later. His penetrating analysis of the ills of Israelite society and his magnificent demand for moral reconstruction are voiced in language of thundering power and poetic beauty that is still overwhelming today, even in translation. It is hard for an honest person to doubt that the authentic voice of God echoes through the words of Amos.

The prophetic movement whose earliest surviving document is the Book of Amos continued for nearly four centuries. It is well known that great personalities and geniuses have appeared in large numbers during certain "golden ages" of culture — the Periclean age of Athens, the Elizabethan period, the generation of the Founding Fathers in America. Rarely, however, have such periods of efflorescence lasted for as long as three hundred years.

Moreover, these golden ages usually coincided with times of political and economic prosperity. Sometimes the cultural flowering outlasted the material success, but not as a rule for more than a few generations. But the prophetic movement was launched on the eve of national disintegration and continued gloriously long after the national life was utterly smashed. Thus even in terms of cultural history, the appearance of so many spiritual and literary geniuses is an anomaly. There were, moreover, other great prophets whose words have not survived (we know the names of one or two of them), and it is probable that we have only a small part of what the prophets we know actually taught. Add to this the fact, which we have previously demonstrated, that the prophetic teaching was altogether different from and infinitely superior to anything we find in the whole culture of the ancient Near East — and the magnitude of the phenomenon is heightened still further.

The adherents of modern liberal religion profess the theory of "progressive revelation." They believe, that is, that the truth of God is made manifest through the continuing search of all men for enlightenment and goodness. All the scientists, poets, philosophers and religious teachers are the channels of God's revelation to mankind. But we know now that even biological evolution does not proceed by gradual, almost imperceptible steps, such as Darwin postulated. Evolution is a discontinuous process, which sometimes seems to lapse into stagnation, then moves ahead by sudden unpredictable jumps. If we accept the notion of a progressive revelation even as a working hypothesis, then the advances recorded in the Hebrew Bible constitute the most extraordinary mutation in the entire history of spiritual evolution.

We shall not attempt a more complete theological justification of the prophets' claim that God spoke to and through them. But of this much we can be sure. The prophets were neither dishonest nor psychopathic. They were men of extraordinary intellectual, moral, and esthetic gifts who lived in an age not yet so sophisticated as to indulge in elaborate self-analysis. They never doubted that the powerful religious insights they experienced came to them from God. We may hesitate to dogmatize as to how their message came to them: but it was a message that would have been worthy for God to transmit to mankind.

XIII

THE CHOSEN PEOPLE

Finally, we come to the proposition which recurs so often in Scripture, which has often aroused resentment among non-Jews and embarrassed many Jews, the doctrine that God "chose" Israel.

> "How odd
> Of God
> To choose
> The Jews",

remarked a British wit. But annoying or embarrassing or odd, there is a reality here to be faced.

The Bible is the product of the experience of the people of Israel. Whether we judge it in relation to the cultures contemporary with it, or consider its continuing impact on human history, or test its relevance to our own lives, we must acknowledge it to be one of the chief phenomena in the life of mankind. Without it neither Christianity nor Islam is thinkable. Thus the election of ancient Israel is not a controversial theory, but a historical datum.

This datum of itself does not explain how the election occurred. It does not exclude the possibility that there were or are other chosen peoples. It does not of itself guarantee that the Jewish people are still chosen. Orthodox Christians firmly believe that God chose Israel of old, but they hold that this election was nullified when the Jews rejected the Christian savior.

Whether the Jews today are still an elect group cannot be decided on the basis of Biblical writings alone, and we shall not attempt to foreclose the discussion here. We shall only remind the reader briefly how the Biblical writers understood the doctrine of Israel's election.

It was not based on any inherent superiority of the Israelite race. "The Lord did not set His love upon you, nor choose you, because ye were more in number than any people — for ye were the fewest of all peoples — but because the Lord loved you, and because He would keep the oath which He swore unto your fathers" (Deuteronomy 7.7, 8). The election involves a covenant relationship — that is to say, it is contingent on Israel's faithful performance of its responsibility to God: "if ye will hearken unto My voice indeed, and keep My covenant, then ye shall be Mine own treasure from among all peoples" (Exodus 19.5). The election does not grant favors, but imposes obligations; God has a right to expect more of those whom He has chosen: "You only have I known of all the families of the earth, therefore I will visit upon you all your iniquities" (Amos 3.2). And the same prophet makes clear that the choice of Israel does not imply the rejection of other peoples; quite the contrary:

> "Are ye not as the children of the Ethiopians
> unto Me,
> O children of Israel? saith the Lord.
> Have I not brought up Israel out of Egypt,

And the Philistines from Caphtor,
And Aram from Kir?" (Amos 9.7).

And on the highest levels of prophetic thought, the choice of Israel means that Israel is to serve and bless mankind, by witnessing to the one God and to His righteous law before all peoples. This is the sublime message of the Second Isaiah. We shall quote only one of many pertinent passages; but it may be enlightening first to quote another utterance concerning a chosen people. This is how Vergil states the "mission" of Rome:

"Others may chisel breathing statues of bronze more skillfully, I doubt not, or fashion living features from marble; they may plead causes more eloquently, delineate the movements of the heaven and number the rising stars. Thou, O Roman, be mindful that thou must sway the peoples by thy power. These shall be thy arts: to impose the terms of peace, to spare those who humble themselves and to crush in war the proud" (Aeneid 6:848–854).

But the prophet speaks in God's name to Israel:

"I the Lord have called thee in righteousness,
And have taken hold of thy hand,
And kept thee, and set thee for a covenant of the
    people,
For a light of the nations;
To open the blind eyes,
To bring out the prisoners from the dungeon,
And them that sit in darkness out of the prison-
    house" (Isaiah 42.6, 7).

And in this mission of liberation and enlightenment, the Bible itself has served grandly.

Our final conclusion as to what is the word of God and whether the Jews are a chosen people may be affected by reading Scripture, but must ultimately be a decision of personal faith. But whatever opinions we may form concerning that phenomenon called the Hebrew Bible, we can ill afford to disregard it.

XIV

THE MESSIAH

The Jewish teachings regarding the Messiah are a subject of great interest to both Jews and Christians, and at times also a subject of much confusion. The idea of the Messiah underwent extensive development in post-Biblical times; indeed it is no longer possible to discuss Jewish messianism intelligibly without reference to these later developments. But the roots of the idea are to be found in the Hebrew Bible; and it is to the Bible we must turn first in order to understand the Jewish messianic hope.

Biblical thinking is oriented to the future. Whatever importance we attach to the Paradise story, as told in Genesis 2–3, the other Biblical writers seldom refer to it. In a few passages, Eden is mentioned as a symbol of fertile, beautiful country; but nowhere in the Bible is there a lament for the lost Eden or an expressed hope of returning to it. Instead, the Biblical authors look forward to a future that will exceed anything the past has shown. They depict this future, sometimes in terms of Israel's national glory, sometimes in broader terms of a united mankind.

Such visions are found both in the Torah and the prophets. In the Pentateuch the pattern is usually a lengthy and grim account of the punishments that the people will suffer for disobedience of God's law, followed by a briefer assurance of forgiveness and restoration when the chastened people turns back to God. In some versions, the spiritual renewal and political restoration will be initiated by God, in order to fulfill His promises to the patriarchs. (See Leviticus 26, Deuteronomy 4, 30, 32).

Many prophetic writings present a similar pattern in which predictions of national catastrophe are followed by promises of ultimate redemption. Those prophets, however, who lived after the calamities had taken place concentrated chiefly on the message of hope.

These messages of hope sometimes depict an ideal future, a Golden Age to come, when righteousness, justice, and peace shall prevail everywhere. Several of these center around the figure of a king under whose leadership the era of universal goodness will be inaugurated and maintained. The chief passages are Isaiah 9.1–6, 11.1–10, and 32. Scholars disagree as to whether Isaiah himself wrote them. If he did, chapter 9 might be understood not as a vision of the future, but as a declaration that the new era has begun—perhaps with the advent of King Hezekiah to the throne. But many authorities (with whom the present writer is inclined to agree) consider these sections later than the time of Isaiah and understand them as predictions of a better time that lies ahead.

The clearest account is given in chapter 11. The hoped-for ruler is to be a descendant of David's family. He will be endowed with the highest qualities of mind and spirit: wisdom, understanding, might, and reverence. He will champion the cause of the weak and downtrodden. He will not be deceived by appearances, and his decisions will be wholly just. He will not need to use brutal or bloody methods of enforcing his will: his powerful words will be a sufficient rod to chastise the wicked. Wrong will be swept away, ferocity replaced by gentleness—"the wolf shall go to dwell with the lamb." The whole earth will be full of the sense of God's presence, as the waters fill the sea.

This ideal ruler of the future is often referred to as the Messiah. Indeed, the term "messianic" is often applied to such prophecies as Isaiah 2.2–4, where a future of peace and brotherhood is depicted even though no Messiah is mentioned. This word Messiah has a curious and fascinating history.

The Hebrew verb *mashach* means "to smear with oil." Ancient Israelite rulers were formerly inducted into office by the rite of pouring olive oil upon their heads. This practice is mentioned chiefly with reference to the inauguration of kings, though the anointment of prophets and priests is also mentioned in several places.* In short, anointing was roughly equivalent to coronation; and the term "anointed one" *(mashiach,* whence ultimately our word messiah) was essentially a royal title.

The Bible never uses this title without qualification. The Israelite king is called "the anointed of the Lord"; but a pronominal suffix ("My anointed," "His anointed") is used to indicate the same notion. This usage, Kaufmann Kohler once argued, implies a denial of the belief widely held among ancient peoples that the king was an incarnate deity. The kings of Israel were the anointed agents of God, from whom alone they derived their authority.

In various Biblical passages David is represented as calling King Saul "the anointed of the Lord;" elsewhere he speaks of himself as "the anointed of the God of Jacob"—meaning the same thing. (See I Samuel 24.7, II Samuel 23.1). Later books make occasional reference to the anointed one. Sometimes the reference is to an actual ruler, who is not named

---

*A few passages also use the verb *mashach* in cases where oil was used to consecrate various objects for religious purposes. The word always has a ceremonial significance. An entirely different verb is used to indicate the rubbing of the body with oil for the sake of cleanliness—a common practice among the ancients who lacked our abundance of soap and water.

and cannot be specifically identified (Lamentations 4.20, Psalm 89.39, 52). Sometimes the allusion seems to be to a future ruler from the Davidic family (Psalm 2.2) or to the people of Israel as personified by its king (Habbakuk 3.13). One Psalm (105.15, repeated in I Chronicles 16.22) calls the patriarchs "God's anointed ones." In one extraordinary passage (Isaiah 45.1) the great prophet of the exile applies this title to the Persion conqueror Cyrus—as much as to say that foreign rulers also are the appointed agents of the universal God worshipped by Israel. These variations do not obscure the simple fact that in the Bible the expression "anointed of the Lord" is a royal title, applied in particular to the Davidic kings.

This term does not appear in the prophetic descriptions of the ideal future ruler. It was in post-Biblical times that men began to speak of the messiah (sometimes the term used is *melek ha mashiach*, the anointed king) in the sense of a future king whose advent is eagerly awaited. This term summed up the hopes of the people both for national independence and for a nobler and happier social order. The messiah was contrasted on the one hand with the foreign tyrants—Chaldean, Persian, Hellenistic, Roman—who ruled Palestine and its people. On the other, he was contrasted with the unworthy native kings who had once ruled Israel and Judah. The day would come, people believed, when God would restore the dynasty of David in the person of a good king; this king would free them from foreign oppression and set up an order of justice and peace in their land and even throughout the world. This hope is still expressed in the traditional prayers of the Synagogue.

In tracing this development, we have gone beyond the frame of the Hebrew Bible. The development had two aspects. Most people looked forward to the appearance of a national liberator who would free his own people and subjugate the heathen empires. But some unpolitical seers envisioned the messiah as a quasi-angelic being, waiting in heaven for the time appointed for him to descend, manifest his power, and reign as God's agent on earth.*

At the beginning of the Christian era, Roman rule was bitterly resented by most of the Jews of Palestine, and the repressive policies of the Roman governors roused messianic expectations to a high pitch. Jesus of Nazareth was one of several popular figures around whom such expectations centered. (It is difficult to determine whether he himself claimed to be the messiah). Because they regarded him as an actual or potential leader of revolt, he was crucified

---

*This is the picture found in the extra-Biblical Book of Enoch, which calls the messiah "the son of man." In Ezekiel, this term meant simply "mortal." Later it became a messianic title, and appears as such frequently in the New Testament. In Daniel 7.13, the one "like unto a son of man" is probably not the messiah, but the personification of the Jewish people.

by the Roman officials, who inscribed on his cross the words "King of the Jews."

To the average Jew it was evident that Jesus was not the messiah, since he had failed to liberate his people from Rome. (Even those who invested the messiah with heavenly qualities still expected him to bring earthly deliverance!) But a group of his devoted followers clung to the faith that he was indeed the messiah; they were therefore forced to adopt a radically new concept of the messiah's character and function. They continued to use the title "anointed" (in Hebrew, *mashiach;* in Aramaic, *meshicha;* in Greek, *christos*); but though the word was old, the meaning was new. For the Jews who adhered to tradition, the messiah was essentially a human ruler who would reign in this world. For the followers of Jesus, the messiah or christ was literally divine, an aspect of the godhead, who had become incarnate in human form, and whose death and resurrection provided men with a means of salvation from sin and death.

Thus the often heard statement that Jews still await the messiah, while Christians believe he has come already, fails to describe the real facts. First, because Jews mean by the term messiah something quite different from what Christians mean by the term Christ. Second, because the question of the messiah is central in Christianity (as the very name implies), while in Judaism the belief in the messiah, though important, is not fundamental. Large segments of modern Jewry no longer await the coming of a personal messiah. They look forward rather to the "messianic age"—described, for example, in Isaiah 2—as the ideal toward which mankind in general and the Jewish people in particular must strive. The Zionist movement is one of several modern reinterpretations of the messianic hope of Judaism.

We have gone far beyond the Hebrew Bible, but with good reason. For Christianity, which accepted the Hebrew Scriptures as authoritative, claimed to find in these writings many prophetic anticipations of the messianic career of Jesus. As a result, numerous passages in the Bible which Jewish tradition has not understood as messianic, have been so interpreted by Christian apologists.

The most famous, perhaps, is Isaiah 7. It concerns a threatened attack on Judah in 734-733 B. C. E. Isaiah assures King Ahaz that the aggressors will not succeed; they will be overwhelmed by Assyria before a baby soon to be born will be old enough to say "mama" and "papa." To celebrate this deliverance, the child will be named Immanuel ("God is with us"). The mother of the child is referred to as an *almah* ("young woman"); the mistranslation of this word as "virgin" led Christian believers to take the passage as a prophecy of the birth of Jesus seven centuries later. Jewish interpreters never regarded the chapter as messianic; and many responsible Christian scholars today accept this view.

Several passages in the latter part of Isaiah describe in exalted terms the career and character of "the servant of the Lord." The most remarkable of these (Isaiah 52.13–53.12) represents the servant as enduring suffering even to death, with the result that mankind attains to healing and redemption. Christians have generally understood this chapter as foretelling the redemptive suffering of Jesus.

The identity of the "servant of the Lord" is still the subject of scholarly debate. Jewish tradition has generally regarded the servant as the personification of the people of Israel, which must undergo many trials in the fulfillment of its mission (cf. above p. 93). This view is held today by many Jewish and non-Jewish interpreters. Others have supposed that the servant was an actual prophet—Jeremiah, perhaps, or even Deutero-Isaiah himself. A few Jewish interpreters, apparently under Christian influence, adopted the notion that the messiah must endure suffering before he can liberate Israel, and have explained Isaiah 53 as messianic; but this interpretation was not widely adopted. Some Christian scholars, we should add, while agreeing that the original reference of the passage is to the Jewish people, still hold that its full meaning was revealed only through the passion of the Christian savior.

Many other passages in the Hebrew Bible have been similarly interpreted. In particular, Christological meanings have been discovered in some difficult and cryptic verses, where it is probable that the text is corrupt—e.g., Genesis 49.10, Psalm 2.12, and Psalm 110.

XV

TEXT AND TRANSLATIONS

The inquiring student may still ask: Just what am I reading when I open a copy of the Bible?

We have seen that it is a collection of books, and that some of these books are themselves composite. Their general character and approximate dates have already been indicated. But how did these ancient writings come down to us? To what extent are the books in our possession identical with what the prophets and sages wrote? What is the nature and validity of the translations we customarily utilize?

Some partial answers have already been given; they can now be made more precise.

I. The Text

Much of the Biblical material consists of sayings, songs, stories, and laws that were transmitted orally for a long time before being put into written form. The actual writing was done in ink on sheets of parchment or papyrus. Other sections were written or dictated at once by their authors, or were compiled from older written documents. In a few instances, materials may have been adapted or translated from other languages, and may have originally been inscribed on clay or stone tablets.

As the Biblical books grew, separate sheets were

stitched together into rolls. The Torah scrolls used in the service of the Synagogue preserve this ancient form; but the wooden rollers, as well as the covers and ornaments that now bedeck the scroll, are later refinements. During the Middle Ages, scrolls were replaced—except for ritual purposes—by manuscripts bound in the book form we employ today.

Hebrew Bible manuscripts were not permitted to sleep on library shelves; they were constantly read and studied. Old copies which wore out were replaced by new ones. Consequently, existing Bible manuscripts are relatively late: until recently, the oldest known manuscript of the Hebrew Bible was one dating from the ninth century, whereas there are copies of Greek and Syriac translations some five centuries older.

Ancient manuscripts, like the Torah-scrolls today, contained only the consonantal text: the vowels had to be supplied by the reader. The little markings above and below the consonants which now denote the vowel sounds for the unskilled reader were invented by scholars known as the Masoretes, i.e. students of the tradition (*Masorah*). The Masoretes worked in Palestine and Babylonia between the seventh and tenth centuries. In addition to indicating the vowels, they also provided punctuation marks which serve both as a guide to the sense and as notation for the traditional chanting of the various books.

The Masoretes are often credited with standardizing the Bible text. We have seen that manuscripts of the Hebrew Bible are all very much alike, variant readings being relatively few and unimportant. This amazing degree of uniformity is no accident; it is not to be found in any other ancient work of which many manuscript copies exist. In fact, however, the medieval Masoretes only *completed* the work of standardization. The Talmudic literature, which is centuries older than the Masoretic works, is full of Bible quotations which almost always agree with our present readings. (The Talmudic discussions often turn on the exact form and even spelling of a word in the Bible.)

The caves near the Dead Sea have yielded a number of Biblical scrolls which many scholars date from about the beginning of the Christian era. If this dating is correct, these texts are many centuries older than any previously known Bible manuscripts. But the discoveries have not brought about any revolution in Biblical studies. Some of the scrolls contain a consonantal text virtually identical with the Masorah. Others present a number of minor variations, together with some oddities of spelling; they appear to be careless and unreliable copies of a text much like that of our tradition.

For a convincing witness to a Bible text significantly different from our present one, we must turn to the old Greek translation, known as the Septuagint. Its first parts were probably made in the third century B.C.E., and the work of translation probably extended over a century and a half. The Alexandrian Jews who produced this translation arranged the books in an order that seemed to them more correct than the one found in Hebrew manuscripts. This order has been followed by Christian translators, even when their rendering is based on the Hebrew text; but modern Jewish translators have adhered to the arrangement of books in the Hebrew Bible.

The Greek translation, or Septuagint, eventually included a number of Jewish writings not found in the Hebrew Bible. Most of these writings were taken over into the Latin Vulgate, the official Scripture of the Roman Catholic Church. (The Vulgate also contains one interesting work, 4 Esdras, of which both the Hebrew original and the Greek translation have been lost.) The Catholic Old Testament is therefore more extensive than the Jewish Bible or the Protestant Old Testament. The additional books include the two Books of the Maccabees, Tobit, the Wisdom of Solomon, the Wisdom of Ben Sira, and other valuable documents. These writings have often been published separately as the Apocrypha (hidden books).

The important point is that in many places, the Septuagint appears to have been based on a Hebrew text quite different from the Masorah.

This does not mean that every rendering in the Greek that differs from what we might have expected implies a different Hebrew text. Sometimes

the Greek translators made mistakes; sometimes they
followed an old tradition that departed from the
literal sense; and sometimes they seem to have tried
to "improve" upon the original. But often it is plain
that their Hebrew manuscripts were quite different
from ours. In the Book of Jeremiah, the arrangement of the chapters in Greek is entirely different
from that of the Hebrew, and the Greek Job is
considerably shorter than the original. Sometimes
the variants of the Greek are inferior to the Hebrew
text; sometimes they make better sense and are
probably closer to what the author intended.*

There are in fact many passages in the Bible that
are obscure and probably corrupt. Jewish and
Christian fundamentalists will insist on dogmatic
grounds that the inspired text is above criticism; but
all other students recognize that the writings we
possess are not always identical with what the
authors wrote. Between the time of their composition and the time when they were recognized as
sacred books and watched with special care, they
were copied and recopied. Mistakes were bound to
creep in. A letter was misread; a word or line was

---

*An interesting example of this is I Samuel 14.41, where
the Hebrew text is manifestly incomplete, and the translation
"Declare the right" is a guess. The Greek reads here: "And
Saul said, O LORD God of Israel, why have You not an-
swered your servant today? If the guilt is in me or in my
son Jonathan, give Urim; but if You say that it is in Your
people Israel, give Thummim." (Cf. Exodus 28.30, Numbers 27.21.)

omitted, repeated, or misplaced; errors were sometimes "corrected" by worse errors. Accidents might cause the loss or misplacement of leaves; certain portions might be torn or blotted. Sometimes a scribe might deliberately change a phrase to render it more acceptable to the theological outlook or the standards of taste of his own time.

Such accidents befell all ancient books. But in editing Homer, Cicero, or the New Testament, the errors of one manuscript can be corrected by the readings of other manuscripts. The Hebrew texts of the Bible are, however, virtually all alike, the incorrect readings having been standardized along with the correct ones. Thus the chief resource of the modern scholar who wants to go back of the Masoretic text is the study of the Septuagint. By re-translating the Greek into Hebrew, he can sometimes recover a Hebrew reading preferable to what we have in our Bibles.

The other ancient versions provide only occasional help, for they are either dependent on the Greek or based on a Hebrew text very close to our own. For this reason, when the Greek offers no satisfactory clue to a baffling Hebrew passage, modern scholars have often amended the text by conjecture.*

---

*For example, the traditional translation of Amos 6.12 is "Do horses run upon the rock? Doth one plow there with oxen?" But the second sentence is a makeshift: the word "there" is not found in the Hebrew, which literally means "Doth one plow with oxens (*sic*)?" By dividing the last

Experts are by no means in agreement as to the instances where emendation is necessary or desirable, and as to the relative merit of the various emendations proposed. Jewish scholars have not hesitated to make such changes in the text when speaking or writing as individuals; but translations made under quasi-official Jewish auspices have always adhered closely to the Masorah.

II. Translations

The Septuagint is important to us, not only for purposes of text-criticism, but also because it is our most ancient witness to the tradition of understanding the Scriptures. The Bible contains a number of Hebrew words whose meaning can no longer be determined with assurance. The renderings of such words in the Greek Bible (perhaps based on guesswork, perhaps on old tradition) have often been followed by subsequent translators in many languages.

A notable instance concerns the Divine Name. In the Hebrew Bible, God is often called by a name spelled YHWH. From an early date this name was

Hebrew word into two, without changing a letter, we get "Doth one plow the sea with oxen?"

Ezekiel 3.12 reads, "I heard behind me the sound of a great rustling: 'Blessed be the glory of the LORD from his place!'" A change of one letter, first suggested by the pious traditionalist Samuel David Luzzatto, yields: "I heard behind me the sound of a great rustling, as the glory of the LORD rose from its place."

considered too sacred for ordinary use, and we do not know exactly how it was pronounced. In the Greek, it is regularly rendered by *Kyrios*, the Greek for "Lord." This is precisely the tradition followed by Jews in reading the Hebrew Bible: they substitute *Adonai* ("Lord") wherever they find YHWH in the text.

For several centuries, Greek-speaking Jews viewed the Septuagint with the same awe that English readers have often given to the "King James Version." But this Greek version was later adopted as the standard Scripture of the rising Christian community; some of the inexact renderings it contains were used to bolster Christian claims, and the Jews were even accused of falsifying the Hebrew manuscripts. Jews therefore produced new Greek translations for their own use, which followed more closely the increasingly standardized Hebrew text. Portions of these have survived; one of them—ascribed to the proselyte Aquila—is more like an "interlinear crib" than a translation. But even the Septuagint, portions of which are in reasonably good Greek, often followed so closely the idiom and sentence structure of Hebrew as to produce a strange, exotic effect.

The tradition of understanding the Bible is also reflected in the old Aramaic translations, known as the Targumim. In their present form many of these works are medieval, but they contain ancient elements. Certain of the Targumim are free paraphrases, incorporating lengthy legal and homiletical elaborations. Others, notably the Targum on the Torah which bears the name of Onkelos, are quite literal—except that circumlocutions are used to avoid ascribing human traits to God.

Through the centuries, Jews and Christians alike have discovered in the sacred text legal, moralistic, philosophic, and mystical meanings which would have astonished and baffled the Biblical authors. But a feeling for the plain sense was never lost. During the Middle Ages, formal Hebrew grammar was worked out; thus an instrument was provided for a more systematic and scientific approach to Bible translation. The major effort in this new spirit was the Arabic translation of Rab Saadia Gaon (882–942). Jewish scholars also rendered the Bible into Spanish, but it was usually assumed that the Jew would study his Bible in the original. Many important commentaries and expositions were written in Hebrew. (The eleventh century commentator, Rashi, would occasionally render a difficult word or phrase into French, written in Hebrew characters.) Early Jewish translations into the languages of northern Europe—for instance, into Yiddish—were intended for devotional use by women, and made no pretensions to scholarly exactness.

It was only in the nineteenth century that a sizeable body of Jews appeared who, though possessing general education, could not read the Scriptures in Hebrew. For them reliable translations into modern languages were indispensable.

By the time that a substantial English-speaking

Jewry came into existence, the Bible in English was already an acknowledged classic. The history of the English Bible is far too complicated to be told here. The key figure in the process was William Tyndale (1490 ?-1536), one of the martyrs of the Protestant Reformation, who devoted many years to the translation of both Hebrew and Christian Scriptures. His powerful and rhythmic style was followed in large measure in a series of translations that appeared during the sixteenth century. As none of them seemed entirely satisfactory, King James I appointed a company of learned divines to prepare a new revision.

Their work, published in 1611, has become known as the Authorized Version or "King James Version." Though sharply criticized in some quarters when it appeared, it soon won the whole-hearted acceptance of the devout. It has been widely acclaimed for its literary excellence and sonorous musical quality.

But this translation is clearly unsuitable for Jewish religious use. In a number of places it reads predictions of the Christian savior into the Hebrew text; and the chapter headings with which it is provided are full of Christological interpretations. Yet its prestige was so great and its merits so considerable that Jewish scholars had little desire to attempt something wholly new. Several of the versions produced for Jewish use in England and America in the last two centuries were simply adaptations of the Authorized Version, purged of Christological allusions and of the more obscure archaisms.

Far more independent was the work of Isaac Leeser of Philadelphia (1808–1868). This German-born leader of American Jewry, though busy with many tasks as minister and publicist, was able to produce a careful, sound translation of the Bible, based on the work of medieval and modern Jewish commentators. Leeser attempted to imitate the style of the Authorized Version, but with limited success.

The Christian world, meantime, was having problems with the celebrated and revered translation of 1611. The whole purpose of translating the Bible was to make the sacred word intelligible to the un-learned; the Authorized Version no longer served this purpose. Many words and expressions found there had disappeared from English usage. Other words had undergone considerable change in meaning. (In Tudor English, "prevent" meant "antici-pate," "repent" meant "to change one's mind.") Moreover, continuing progress in Biblical studies had revealed many mistakes and inaccuracies in the King James Bible.

Committees were therefore established in England and the United States to revise the Authorized Ver-sion. The British group published their Revised Version in 1885; in 1901 the American Standard Version appeared, containing many more changes. These revisers did not change the basic style of the King James Bible. They modified the latter only in the interest of accuracy and clarity, and they avoided new words or idioms that would have clashed with the familiar classic style.

The translation issued in 1917 by the Jewish Publication Society of America may be fairly described as a Jewish form of the Revised Version. It offers some variant renderings based on Jewish tradition and on new archeological discoveries. But for the most part it adheres to the established manner of the English Bible. Perhaps that is why it was so quickly adopted for Jewish use throughout the English speaking world. Max Margolis, the editor-in-chief of this version, declared: "No translation in the English tongue . . . can be anything but a revision, a revision of the English Bible of 1611, itself a revision. All attempts at modernizing the English Bible must necessarily fail."

Yet even as he wrote, a different opinion was beginning to spread. Readers were no longer at home in Tudor English, and the need was felt for more than a patchwork revision. Tyndale had rendered the Bible into the language of his day. A translation in contemporary English, whatever it might lose in impressive sonority, would speak to today's readers with far more immediacy. Much of what we have come to think of as "Biblical style" (including the thou-forms) are *English* archaisms not implied by the original.

Moreover Bible translators from the days of the Septuagint on have, out of reverence for the original text, followed too closely the sentence structure and idiom of Hebrew. The resultant Hebraisms are another element of the supposed "Biblical style." Actually, an accurate translation is not one in which each word of the original is rendered by the corresponding word in the second language. Often an entire phrase or clause must be translated by a phrase or clause conveying the same meaning.*

The enormous advances of the past fifty years in understanding the Bible and its background likewise have made necessary a fresh approach to the task of translation. As a result, we have had a number of new renderings, first by individuals, and later by official church groups. Though (like the Authorized Version in its time) they have been harshly attacked on theological, scholarly, and literary grounds, they have also evoked enormous interest and enthusiasm, and have greatly stimulated the reading of the Bible.

It was inevitable that the Jewish community would react to this new trend. Again the Jewish Publication Society of America undertook to provide a Bible version for Jewish use, and published a new translation of the Pentateuch in 1963. It is not a revision of the 1917 version, but a fresh rendering into contemporary English, utilizing all available resources, from the insights of Talmudic and medieval Hebrew commentators to the findings of present day archeologists. Work is now proceeding on the other books of the Bible.

---

*For instance, the phrase "God of my salvation" (Psalm 18.47) reproduces exactly the Hebrew construction. But what it means is "God who grants me victory."

The new translation of the Torah, like most earlier efforts, has been received with mingled praise and blame. Its value can be fully determined only after English-speaking Jews have had sufficient time to test it in use.

XVI

SUGGESTIONS FOR FURTHER READING

The purpose of this section is not to provide a systematic bibliography, even of a rudimentary nature, but simply to help the student whose interests are non-technical to advance in his understanding of the Bible. There are many valuable Christian commentaries, introductions, and studies in the field which are readily available in libraries; our list therefore stresses books by Jews, which are not always taken note of.

SOLOMON B. FREEHOF, *Preface to Scripture* (Union of American Hebrew Congregations, Cincinnati 1950) reflects a liberal viewpoint similar to that presented in this book. It gives a more systematic introduction to the Bible, and selections of salient passages from each book, with brief commentary.

JOSEPH H. HERTZ, *The Pentateuch and Haftorahs* (there are several English and American editions) contains a full commentary on the Torah written in a strongly traditional spirit. In complete disagreement with our approach, the late Chief Rabbi of the British Empire argued in this work for the unity, Mosaic authorship, and divine origin of the Pentateuch. This is an instructive example of the method by which religious conservatives defend their position; more important, it is an admirable exposition of the religious and ethical content of the Torah.

The only English commentary by Jews that extends over the entire Bible is that published by the Soncino Press (*The Soncino Books of the Bible*). A number of distinguished scholars participated in this project; the volumes are of unequal merit.

The Holy Scriptures with Commentary (Jewish Publication Society of America) includes thus far volumes on Numbers, Deuteronomy, Micah, and Proverbs.

The Jewish Commentary for Bible Readers (Union of American Hebrew Congregations) is planned specifically for the layman, and so far covers I Kings, Psalms, and the "Five Scrolls."

CLAUDE G. MONTEFIORE, *Bible for Home Reading*, an English publication long since out of print, may be available in some libraries. It is outstanding for its sensitive (and often inspiring) interpretation of the religious message of the Bible.

ARTHUR S. PEAKE's one-volume *Commentary on the Bible* (New York, 1919; a "Supplement" was published in 1936) is antiquated in spots and in others displays some Christian bias; but it is still a highly useful reference work.

WILLIAM F. ALBRIGHT, *The Archaeology of Palestine* (Penguin Books, 1949) is an authoritative summary of the subject. The most reliable compendium of the ancient oriental writings relevant to the Bible is that mentioned in the body of our work, *Ancient Near Eastern Texts Relating to the Old Testament*, edited by James B. Pritchard (Princeton University Press, 1950); but the amateur will find it easier to consult George A. Barton, *Archeology and the Bible* (American Sunday School Union, revised 1937).

A recent summary of Biblical history is *Ancient Israel* by Harry M. Orlinsky (Cornell University Press 1954).

A convenient and inexpensive edition of the *Apocrypha* is that of Robert H. Pfeiffer (Harper, N. Y. 1953).